Life as a Spectrum Mom

The Ups, Downs, and Upside Downs

of

Parenting Autistic Kids

by

Karen Pellett

Christine
Thank you for
your tremendous feedback
& your friendship
love ys
Karen

Life as a Spectrum Mom
Copyright © 2017 by Karen Pellett
All rights reserved.

ISBN-13: 978-0692888827
ISBN-10: 0692888829

Interior Book Design: Bob Houston eBook Formatting

Dedication

To my children. Thank you for teaching me to see the world in a new light and for helping me to become more than I ever dreamed.

And to every parent who feels like they're alone—you are not alone.

Foreword

I'm going to let you into a world that you thought you knew. Unless you've traveled its path, you might have only caught a hint at this world. That hint might have formed into a thought, an opinion, that may have formulated into an idea, but let me tell you and never forget: It was only a glimpse. If you've wondered what it is like to raise an autistic child, I will paint you a picture with the help of my family. We are not every autistic family. We are our own version, carved out of time, trial, and trust. If you are a parent of autistic children, I take you into my heart and hopefully show you that you are not alone.

Contents

Section One:

Winging Mommyhood

Chapter One

Our World

I told my daughter a secret: In my opinion 90 percent of the time, 100 percent of people don't get their way. The beauty of being a kid is that it's all about practice. You get to make all your mistakes now, so that you've figured it all out by the time you're an adult.

When I was a child, I dreamed of being a mom. I would marry soon after college, then settle down to family life. I would be the type of mother glorified in sitcoms like *Happy Days* and *The Brady Bunch*. I would have four children—two boys and two girls—blessedly spaced three years apart to ensure adequate time to adjust to each child's personality before bringing another life into the world. Then, my husband and I would raise our children with wisdom and understanding. Sure, there would be chaos; a family wouldn't be a family without it, but I would be "inspired" to know just how to help my children through those turbulent times. In the end, our children would grow up to be responsible, caring, and respectful adults.

Ha.

My reality has been far different than I could have foreseen. For one, I missed my pre-established idea of when I'd get married by over six years. For another, when I did get married, I became the instant stepmom of two amazing, rambunctious boys who lived with their mother in another state. Let me tell you, any type of parenting from a distance is nigh impossible. It was another six years and an exhausting and costly amount of fertility treatments before we had our daughter, Rebekah. One move, twenty-two months, and a long bedrest later, our son Colin was born. When I went for a checkup ten months later, I told the doctor that I wanted to have one more child, but they had to be further apart. I was already struggling with being a mom of two kids under three.

Guess what? I was already pregnant with Joseph.

Then, one month into the pregnancy, my husband lost his job due to cutbacks.

I sobbed. It was more than I could handle. I truly felt like a horrible mother already—how could I handle a third child? But silver linings often come in unexpected ways. Having my husband out of work for the majority of the pregnancy was a surprising blessing. Frank was able to help take care of Rebekah and Colin while I took care of myself and the baby growing inside of me. Seven weeks prior to Joseph's due date, my husband went back to work, and I ended up in the hospital with preeclampsia.

The kids had to spend their days at a friend's house while my husband worked, and I lay in the hospital for a week of hospitalization and three more of strict bedrest. A stressed-out momma does not help the family, but I could not fix this. My world was tumbling out of control, and I had to lay there and watch. Thankfully, Joseph was born healthy and tenacious, but the doctor informed me it was too risky for me to ever be pregnant again. So, after at least two thousand heparin shots, one thousand insulin shots and pills, four miscarriages, two hundred metformin pills, two bouts of preeclampsia, and two breech births, my tubes were finally tied. My hopes of having a second girl were lost.

When Frank and I first moved to Utah only two months after our daughter, Rebekah, was born, I didn't have other family members nearby to aid in times of distress—like when my six-month-old baby had been crying for three hours straight, and all my calming tactics failed. I called the wife of our local church leader, whom I'd met only briefly, begging for help. The moment she came over, and I placed my daughter into her arms, Rebekah stopped crying. Then, I began crying.

So, when the doctors and specialists told me, "No, it's not you" and "It's not your imagination—there is a problem," I actually felt great relief. I have no doubt there are still many areas regarding motherhood that I sorely need to improve on, but at least, for the moment, the problem wasn't only me.

Rebekah was three, Colin almost two, and Joseph a very energetic one year old, I started to realize that my children might not be quite typical. At first, I thought my daughter might have a hearing problem, but the audiologist quickly determined that her hearing was fine; however, he did observe that it seemed as though her brain was not processing what her ears were taking in. Our family physician diagnosed her with Sensory Processing Disorder.

I quickly became inundated with occupational therapist appointments and the complicated process of testing and enrolling my daughter in an early intervention preschool program. My sons soon showed indications of atypical behavior and were signed up for a local at-home program for developmentally delayed children. When Colin first began his sessions, the specialists warned me that he showed all the early warning signs of being on the autism spectrum. Thus, I began group therapy appointments for moms needing aid in understanding and accepting that their children would never be "normal."

I was relieved to discover my children had typical behavior for an atypical situation. I had previously come to the conclusion that the struggles we were experiencing were a direct result of my being a horrible mom—that somehow, I'd missed the day motherhood skills were handed out to all women. The hospital sends you home with loads of information of how to take care of your child, but the manual on mother's instinct and how to handle children once their personalities kicked in was missing in my take-home packet.

With the building signs of autism and the realization that atypical behavior would be typical for our family, I came to the quick conclusion that, even though I desperately longed for another child, my hands were more than full. I made the decision to muddle through until I learned to be a better mom. I even modified my own behavior to deal with the stress. If we needed something from the store, I would drive to the store with all three kids, but it had to be a store that had, what I called, "child carts." Then, I would drive around the parking lot until I found a cart. If a cart was available, no matter how far away from the store, I'd park next it, click the kids into the safety of their seat belted ride, and then brave grocery shopping. If no child carts were to be found outside, I went home.

I also learned that our kids could not go out front to play unless my husband was home with us. We were still outnumbered two to three, but at least we were more likely to keep the children out of danger. Because the moment the kids went outside, they bolted in opposite directions. Rebekah would run like a hare, soaking up all the sensory detail around her. Colin would start testing all our neighbors' door knobs until he found one unlocked. Then he'd help himself to investigating their house—all things in *his* world are open for exploration. Boundaries were not a concept he understood. Then, there was Joseph, who'd run straight into the street without hesitation or fear to chase a butterfly or get to grandma's house.

This was our norm. We'd learn to adapt as needed along the way.

But when we saw other kids playing, we realized that our children's typical behaviors were not typical to everyone else around us. The search for answers was long road with repetitive testing through the school system and medical professionals and a plethora of opinions from loved ones and friends. I was overwhelmed. Then, when Joseph turned five, he was diagnosed with social and communications disorders (previously identified as symptoms of Asperger's syndrome), developmental delays, and aggressive tendencies. But through that diagnostic process, we also learned that my husband has attention deficit disorder (ADD) and that I have

Figure 1 – The Pellett Family - Halloween 2015

SPD and ADHD just like my daughter. Throw in a few white matter brain lesions in atypical multiple sclerosis locations the doctors identified when my kid threw a car seat at my head, and, well, you get the picture. Life is more than a bit crazy.

Is it hard? Yes.

Is it worth enduring? Absolutely—at least that is what I want to say most days.

No, it was not my childhood dream, but I had two healthy boys, a healthy girl, two amazing stepsons that we lived a lot closer to, and a patient husband who loved me in spite of it all. I thought the difficult part of my journey was over.

As a family, we are far from normal. The beauty of that is that we are learning that it is okay. Every family has its struggles. Every family is unique. Ours may be a tad more insane from time to time, filled to the brim with loads of learning, and, sometimes, even a little dark around the edges. And yes, a little counseling along the way has helped a ton.

Stories like this happen in spectrum families all over the world, but they are all unique with their own twists and turns. But this story is ours. Welcome to our world—please wipe your feet on the way in.

Chapter Two

Kids' Stats

Being a mom of autistic kids feels like they are speaking Chinese while all I have is a German-English translation dictionary.

Baseball cards often offer statistics for the player featured on the card that include details like runs scored, batting average, and so on. These details provide the fans with important facts that help flush out the players' skills and history, thus painting a more complete picture of their abilities.

In honor of my love of the Boston Red Sox and Seattle Mariners (my husband is a fifth- generation Chicago Cubs fan, poor thing), I am including stats regarding our children, their diagnoses, and their personalities. The stories and anecdotes in this book will then come to life more fully for you as you read. Keep in mind that all three of my kids were born within three and a half years, and though diagnoses and definitions have changed over the years, my kids have not.

The pediatric developmental specialist that diagnosed our children once told me, "If you only had one special needs child you would have *this* [indicating my child] covered. You'd be a pro. The difficulty is that you have three kids with different types of special needs. Because of that, they trigger each other's triggers. I'm just impressed you aren't more of a mess."

Without further ado, I give you my children:

Portrait of My Sensory Child

Name: Rebekah

Diagnoses: Attention-deficit/hyperactivity disorder (ADHD), sensory processing disorder (SPD), anxiety

Favorite Animal: Giraffe

Favorite Color: Pink

Favorite Food: Pepperoni Pizza, Burger King Zesty Dipping Sauce (not together, thank goodness).

Food Aversions: Any meat other than chicken nuggets or pepperoni on pizza, any vegetable ever created except French fries and ketchup.

Figure 2 - Rebekah's scorpion fish

Favorite Drink: "Mommy's soda, because I love you, Mommy."

Favorite TV Shows: *Bill Nye the Science Guy*, *Wild Kratts*, *Odd Squad*

Favorite Music: Jazz (because mommy likes jazz)

Favorite Activities: Drawing scorpion fishes (part tiger, part lion, part shark, part scorpion), reading foreign language dictionaries and joke books, and performing candy science experiments.

Dreams/Aspirations: To run a zoo in Florida (because the host of one of her favorite Happy Kids TV shows lives there).

Talents: Math, science, funny quips, running, and near perfect recall of anything in her long-term memory

Triggers: Air, noise, colors, lights, people, the door, band-aids, the television, her brothers, forgetting, not winning and anything that messes with her routine or expectations.

Coping Techniques: Enclosed spaces—since she could crawl, Rebekah has found comfort in tight spaces. If she is upset, a good bear hug will help put a smile on her face. One of her favorite sports was to remove all the DVDs from our entertainment unit, crawl into the cupboard and close the door behind her. During the terrible twos stage, she transitioned into using a play tent or tunnel as her safety reset zone. Now she commandeers empty boxes, fills them with stuffed animals, and dives in. More often than not, after a rough day I will find her fast asleep, snuggled with her stuffed pets, a book still opened to where she'd left off before drifting into dreamland. Also, when she is really struggling to focus, the best thing for Rebekah is movement—she needs to jump, run, wrestle, tumble, and slide, in order to calm her body down enough for her mind to work.

Figure 3 - Rebekah at eight years old

Mommy Summation: Rebekah rolled over at three days old, while still in the hospital. The family doctor did not believe us until she came in to check on our baby, and Rebekah rolled over for her. Our daughter has been our Energizer Bunny, running everywhere since. Because of her SPD, Rebekah often leaps off of high ledges or runs into walls/doors on purpose in order to trigger the same mental sensation I would have hopping in place. If too many of her senses are triggered at once, her brain is unable to process what data it is receiving and she shuts down as a protection measure. For example, if the ceiling fan is blowing on her skin while she is reading a book, she literally *cannot* hear me talking to her from six inches away.

Figure 4 - Rebekah climbing over banister at two years old

Also because of the ADHD and SPD, Rebekah's mind processes information at an extremely low rate. In mommy terms, think of the movie *50 First Dates*—Rebekah has practically no short-term memory. She is unable to complete chores that include more than one step at a time. She has to achieve the first step before I can explain the next step. However, if she learns a topic in a multi-sensory manner, the knowledge beams right to long-term memory. If that's the case, she will recall a conversation word for word that she and I had three years ago, including what we were doing and what we were wearing.

Rebekah is brilliant when it comes to facts about animals that she learned from watching the PBS Kids show *Wild Kratts* from when she was a toddler. Also, if you put anything to music she will have it memorized. She is stellar when it comes to recalling our phone number, address, and the theme song from every Mario game she's ever played. She has a generous soul, a beautiful heart, and eyes that sparkle when she is happy.

Food is one of Rebekah's biggest issues. She use to eat everything; when she was a baby, I went so far as to make my baby food from scratch and freeze it in ice cube trays (it is a lot easier than you'd expect). But when Rebekah hit two and half years old, the food aversions kicked in. She will gladly eat Kraft mac 'n cheese (freshly made, not reheated), cinnamon chip toast, donuts, pepperoni pizza, grilled cheese sandwiches, chicken nuggets and fries (must be the correct shape), cold cereal (sans milk), and orange juice with no pulp. People have suggested we let her starve until she is willing to eat whatever we make.

Rebekah hates things that interfere with exploring her world, like eating and sleeping. Her pediatrician had us supplement her diet with a special milk of a Carnations Breakfast Essentials High Protein drinks, but Rebekah will only drink the premade French vanilla variety. And once she became used to it, her attitude shifted to, "If I can get all the nutrients I need between this and a vitamin, then why do I have to sit down at the dining table to eat? I can take the drink to go and keep doing what I'm doing." As far as starvation goes, my daughter will happily never eat again if she doesn't have to. If her food isn't visually appealing to her, or if we force her to eat it, she will throw up every single time.

Because of her food aversions, Rebekah has struggled to gain weight as she has gotten older. And trying to find an ADHD medication that doesn't dampen what little desire she has to eat makes it even more difficult. Her doctors are concerned enough that one of them told me, "If she likes pepperoni pizza, then give her pepperoni pizza. At this point she is in desperate need of the calories." Our regular pediatrician even informed Rebekah at her last checkup that if she didn't start gaining weight, we would have to put a tube in her stomach for mommy to feed her. Rebekah is so afraid of needles that he is hoping the threat of a feeding tube will impress upon her the necessity of eating right.

With her processing speed struggles, my daughter does not understand social cues. Give her math and science where there are clearly defined rules, expected results, and processes, and she is a whiz. Give her any variable—like people—and she is utterly confused. Society is full of preconceived ideas and vague expectations that vary from person to person. But Rebekah has found a way to adapt; she takes her cues from the behavior of other individuals she is around. At school, she mimics the behaviors of the other children. When she was in a small special needs class with children more disabled than she is, she would mimic their behavior and would climb on the furniture. And yet, when the kindergarten teacher tested her in an integrated classroom with a resource aide, she followed the example of the other children, sitting at their desks and working on the assignments.

That works well at school, but when she gets home, she is surrounded by her parents and her brothers, who have their own triggers and struggles. Everyone in our household behaves differently, and that messes with her ability to translate what the correct social behavior to follow is. Home is also her safe zone, where she feels free to be herself and knows we will love her no matter what. As a result, chaos tends to ensue when we all get together.

Portrait of my Moderate-Functioning Autistic Child

Name: Colin

Diagnoses: Moderate-functioning (Level 2) autism

Favorite Animal: Frogs

Favorite Color: Green

Favorite Food: Any flavor pancakes as long as it is made from Jiffy mix

Favorite Drink: Milk, AW (like "aw man!" but he really means A&W Root beer)

Favorite TV Shows: *Sesame Street, Pokémon, Thomas & Friends, Chuggington, Dinosaur Train, Big Block Sing Song*

Favorite Music: The Blue Man Group, They Might Be Giants

Figure 5 - Colin's coping technique

Favorite Activities: Anything involving anticipation, any vehicle with wheels, singing, and problem solving.

Dreams/Aspirations: I wish I knew.

Talents: Puzzles, escaping, complex problem solving, perfect recall regarding the order of songs and lists.

Triggers: Screaming/loud noises (especially from his siblings), anything that takes him out of *his* world, insisting that he has to focus on one thing when he is intent on doing another, not getting his way, and anything that messes with his routine or expectations.

Coping Techniques: Lining objects in a row (pots and pans, toy cars, etc.), taking every object out of his toy boxes so that he can see them all spread out on the floor, playing anticipation games I made up when they were little.

Mommy Summation: Colin is a sensory avoider and a sensory seeker wrapped into one dynamic package. From birth, he's found comfort in touch when he can handle it. When he was teething, I would calm him by caressing his cheek. If he struggled to sleep, I would run my thumb up and down his forehead, and he'd fall quickly asleep. And yet this same boy struggles with touch, movement, lights, and sounds from

Figure 6 - Colin at the science museum - 2016

others that bring him out of the world he lives inside. If he is the one making the noise—screaming or dancing around—then he is happy. But if anyone else is making the noise, and Colin is already struggling, he unleashes his inner mixed-martial artist and goes all kung fu on their butts.

Colin is brilliant, but I struggled figuring out how to communicate in a way that we would both understand. When he was four, specialists from an in-home early intervention program sat me on the floor near Colin and taught me to wait. I learned to watch his body language, his signals, and his facial expressions. And then I would wait until he invited me into his world. He rarely made eye contact, and he didn't speak. The few times he would let me into his world were like daisies on the first morning of spring for me, his smiles more precious than diamonds, his words rarer than plutonium (and just as explosive).

Then a miracle happened. I was on my bed matching and folding socks when all three kids came running in my bedroom and jumped on my bed. They grabbed the socks and threw them in the air like snow. I growled and threw a pair of socks at him. I'm not proud of it. But that one burst of frustration turned into the laundry equivalent of a food fight. Colors flew across my bedroom as we dive-bombed each other with whatever mismatched footwear we could find. In the end, we fell in a tumbled heap on my bed, out of breath, but smiles on all of our faces.

Colin (who was about four at the time) rolled on his side, squeezed in for a hug, and without eye contact, said, "I love you."

Those three words filled my soul and sent tears streaming down my cheeks. I didn't dare kiss him or touch him for fear of breaking the spell that hung in the air. My heart was so full. It was the most precious gift in the world. Since then I catch a glimpse of the precious moment, usually when I least expect it, and often with six months separating each glimpse. But in those moments when we connect, I feel whole, like maybe I am doing this mom thing right after all.

In first grade, he was reading on a sixth-grade level. He was a powerhouse at deciphering words through phonetics. And yet, he does not see the value in communication. This world is his playground; every object or individual exists solely to solve a riddle after he has exhausted all other options himself.

His greatest love is the anticipation of what is to come. He loves the
idea of opening a box. He loves

Figure 7 - Colin at eight months old

the anticipation of his favorite
scene in a movie and not the
end reward of reaching that
scene. He would rather play
the moments leading up to it
over and over again. Colin took
apart my laptop when he was
two just to see what was inside, but once he had his answer, he felt no
need to put everything back together. His life is lived in search of
answers to questions only he knows.

With his excitement of exploration comes the difficulty of not
understanding dangerous consequences. Since the world is his
laboratory, he does not see the problems with allowing himself into our
neighbors' houses to explore. If he finds an item of interest, he will pick
up the object and bring it home to play with. When we replaced our
front door—damaged from time and weather—we had to replace the
deadbolt with a lock requiring a key in order to get in or out of our
house to ensure his safety and to limit the number of breaking and
entering incidents.

Colin is the reason I am now a pro at replacing door knobs and
child safety locks. I've changed so many door knobs that Colin
dismantled the knob from his bedroom door, piece by piece, just to find
out why knobs were so fascinating to Mommy. Another time, Colin was
standing in the window of the living room when his face lit up with
excitement. He hopped down from his perch, and raced out into the
backyard, returning with his sister's bicycle (complete with training
wheels) in tow. Pulling the bike up to the front door, Colin balanced

precariously on the seat while reaching for the key that was hanging from a thumbtack high on the wall. Once the treasure was in hand, he hopped down, unlocked the deadbolt, ran out into the grass and retrieved a toy he'd seen.

Running inside, he closed and locked the door before returning the key back to its nest. With a grand gesture, Colin hopped off the bike and turned his dad and I.

"Ta-da!"

I gave him a 9.6 for putting back the key.

Colin's spatial reasoning is extraordinary, making him a whiz with puzzles. When I work a puzzle, I find all the straight-edged pieces to create the border before finding the center pieces. Colin, however, mixes up his method every time; sometimes working diagonally, and other times working from the inside out. When he was in kindergarten, the teachers challenged him by increasing the puzzle difficulty. He would struggle for a bit, but then it was as if everything clicked and he'd start to piece things together, without even looking at the box for direction. Within half an hour, Colin would complete puzzles that his teachers struggled to put together.

Recently, his speech therapist pointed out to me that Colin has his own superpower—the ability to turn off his ears. When he works one-on-one with his paraeducators he is attentive, responsive, and excited. When he returns to the classroom, he is plunged into sensory overload to the point that the sounds and movement are too overwhelming for him to bear.

"If you watch his face, there is a moment where you can see that his brain shuts off his hearing," his speech therapist told me. "After that point, he literally cannot hear anything, including the teacher."

To compensate, the speech therapist requested specialized noise-canceling headphones that link to a microphone headset that his teacher wears. When he wears them, the other children in the class are muted and he can focus on his teacher's voice. Since they implemented this technology, his attention span and learning capability has greatly increased.

Colin is also a master when it comes to creative use of everyday objects. I came out of my room and found an empty jug at my feet. Around the corner I heard him splashing his hands into a filled bathroom sink. For a moment, I thought he'd filled up the sink with water and was soaking his toys again (he likes to drink the water out of them afterward). Yes, he had plugged up the sink, and yes it was filled with liquid, but it was milk, not water. Colin was mid-swig, drinking the milk from a ladle when I'd found him out.

Portrait of My Asperger's Child

Name: Joseph

Diagnoses: Social and communications disorder, Asperger's, developmental delays, aggressive tendencies, heart murmur, unusually large head

Figure 8 - Joseph at five years old

Favorite Animal: Dogs, penguins

Favorite Color: Orange

Favorite Food: Little Caesar's Pepperoni Pizza

Favorite Drink: Orange Ninja (aka Tang)

Favorite TV Show: *Mythbusters*, YouTube Videos

Favorite Music: OK GO

Favorite Activities: Any toy involving chain reactions

Dreams/Aspirations: To fly to the moon

Talents: Physical comedy, construction play (gears, dominos, marble runs, trick race tracks, etc.), making people laugh, and escaping.

Triggers: Colin breathing, Colin being in the room, Colin looking out the same window as Joseph—Joseph's brother is his main trigger. Messing with his routine.

Coping Techniques: Joseph is aggressive, because his mind is faster than the rest of him. He copes by lashing out physically. But as he grows, and his body catches up to his mind, the doctors feel that his coping through aggression will lessen. The rest of the time, Joseph finds comfort in tight places. He loves to hide in the closet, crawl under his bunk bed, or squeeze into cabinets. More than once I have had to help rescue him from being trapped in the kitchen turntable. He finds

Figure 9 - One of Joseph's safe spots

comfort in physical movement. When he's not running, he climbs to the top of the stairs and slides down on his belly or rolls down one bump at a time. Throw in doing every activity at the loudest levels, and he is a happy kid.

Mommy Summation: Joseph has always done things his own way. He works in his time and his style, and he will fight you tooth and nail for what he wants. He is tenacious and adamant and will argue you to death. Joseph and I butt heads a lot, but I chalk that up to his fall birthday giving him an additional year at home with me. Despite that,

I would not give him up for anything in the world. He is my light. He makes me giggle. His bear hugs keep me safe. He is my comedian. When we are home alone in the afternoons before the other kids get home from school, we play Mario Kart together or build Marble Runs and Gears! Gears! Gears! sets. He is always building, whether it is pillow forts or modifications to his brother's Hot Wheels tracks.

On the flip-side, because his mind works faster than his communication abilities, he is frustrated often. And when he's frustrated, he lashes out. In fact, on his third birthday he expressed his frustration by throwing a car seat at my head.

His mind is constantly running, and because of this, he doesn't always hear everything being said to him. To compensate, he'll latch on to one word and create an entire argument in his head based on that single word. When we are

Figure 10 - Joseph at six months old

in the car, he becomes a professional backseat driver and orders me about. When I say, "We are running errands," he starts jumping up and down in his seat and yells, "We're going to Erin's House?"

If I am telling him, "Yes, you can do/have that," he will interrupt, arguing his point about why he should be allowed to have what he wants. Or if you say "not now," he'll ask, "Why not?" even if you are in the middle of explaining that very thing.

Because his mind works faster than his ability to communicate, Joseph finds it easier to act first and pay the piper later. Once we were working as a family to clean the boys' bedroom when Joseph disappeared downstairs. I heard the television and figured he was watching a movie. Ten minutes later I heard a friend come in the house, and say, "Karen, I've got Joseph."

Confused, I did a double take and ran downstairs to find out what had happened. My friend explained that she'd found Joseph crossing the street, and he was nearly hit by a car. As the woman was calling the cops my friend stopped her and said, "I know who he is and where he belongs. I've got this." Joseph explained that he had wanted to go see Grandma and Grandpa, who lived across the street at the time. He had moved several toys in the backyard over to the gate, balanced on top of them, unlatched the gate, and was making his way across the street when my friend found him. He was four years old. I was shaking violently inside for the rest of the day. I thought he was safely ensconced on the couch downstairs and wondered when he'd learned how to maneuver toys, let alone unlatch the back gate. Since then we've kept bungee cords around the gate to prevent such events.

Because of Joseph's quick processing speed, I never know what to expect when it comes to his education. My husband and I are avid readers. We've read to the kids since they were born, and the majority of shows we watch are educational television. When I took Joseph in for his start of school year preschool evaluation his teacher said, "Oh good, he hasn't taught himself to read yet." (His brother had taught himself phonetically, but saw no reason to let anyone know.) When I took Joseph to the dentist for a cleaning a month later, he sat in the chair and read the Subway promotions on signs outside the window out loud.

The startled hygienist turned to me and asked, "How old is he?"

"Five."

"And he's already reading?"

I shrugged and said, "I guess so."

One of Joseph's longtime favorite activities is to watch *Mythbusters* or *Good Eats*. The other day I was working on my laptop on the couch, while Joseph was watching *Mythbusters* and playing with his Marble Run set. I stretched to work out the kinks in my back and couldn't figure out what Adam Savage was holding.

I mumbled, "What is that?"

Joseph replied, "It's a cherry bomb, mom."

Oh crap!

I swear, this kid keeps me laughing, learning, and on my toes.

Chapter Three

The Autism Look

Colin came downstairs dragging Joseph's toddler mattress—totally stripped of all bedding—and started jumping on it. At first, I was going to be mad, then I stopped. The boys were laughing, jumping, happy, and not jumping all over me. Okay, that's a battle I'm happy losing. For now, let them jump.

Once upon a time, or at least a few decades ago, two of my kids might have been diagnosed with Asperger's and the other as autistic. Then, a medical professional far removed from our daily lives, deemed it necessary to lump a large mass of diagnoses under one giant spectrum with sensory issues, ADHD, etc., all being signs or symptoms of the greater label. If you do a search online to try to decipher what autism means today, you will find a myriad of diagrams and explanations that often disagree with one another. In fact, just the other week I was speaking to a doctor from Washington State University that informed me that my son was no longer moderate-functioning autistic; he is now considered Level 2 on the autism spectrum.

Figure 11 - Colin in kindergarten

Say what?

Last I checked, my son is behaving exactly the same as he did a month ago. His routine has not changed. His behaviors have not altered. And his symptoms have not morphed into something new. Another spectrum parent explained to me that the change was to categorize autism based on the level of support or outside aid they require. The medical field, whether for the purpose of cultural sensitivity or for greater clarity on their part, has left a confusing trail of contradictory information for those of us trying to raise these amazing children.

My daughter has ADHD and SPD, but I have yet to find a doctor who will classify her on the current version of the autism spectrum, even though much of my research says that both are signs that an individual might be autistic. In fact, I was driving in downtown Salt Lake City last month and admiring the new billboards popping up around town that say sensory sensitivity is a sign of autism. Well hello—I have two sensory seekers and one mostly-sensory avoider with a touch of seeker hidden in his depths.

Then there are the loving friends and family who say, "Your child doesn't look autistic."

Thanks, I think.

Autism doesn't have a *look* people. Two children the same age placed side by side, both with the exact same diagnosis will often exhibit different behaviors and triggers. Why? Because genetics, history, style of raising, and any number of other variables, all play a factor.

Figure 12 - Rebekah at six years old

If you are a parent of a child or children on the spectrum, please stop judging yourself. Be the best you can be in the moment. What that level is will always change, but as long as you are striving in that moment to do what is best for you and your family then you will always be the best parent you can be.

Another spectrum mom once told me autism is like being color blind: you can't fix being color blind, but you can learn to work around it. A person who is color blind may not see all the colors of a stop light, but they learn that the top circle means stop, the middle means slow down, and the bottom means go.

If that analogy doesn't work for you, try this.

Y r ch ld d sn't l k t st c.

Without the vowels included in the sentence above, you may eventually decipher what I'm trying to say, but it will probably take you longer, and you might have to create your own set of rules regarding language so that this puzzle makes sense. It does not change the fact that the vowels are missing, but you eventually learn the message.

Your child doesn't look autistic.

You cannot judge my kids' behaviors by another autistic child's behaviors. And I should not judge your children by mine. Each child's world is their own, and an autistic child can often get lost in that world. So please stop. Stop making instant judgments when you see a mom

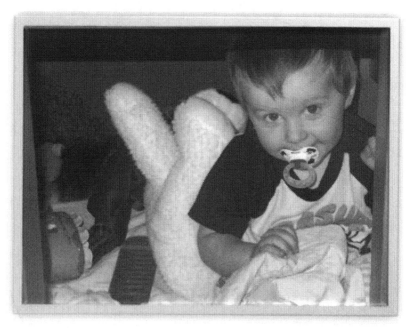

Figure 13 - Joseph at 21 months

struggling to "contain" her children in the doctor's office. Stop assuming because something worked for one friend then it *has* to work for another. Instead, pull up a piece of floor and watch. Observe the beauty of the children before you, and if you are lucky, they might just let you into their world. If you get a glimpse into their world everyone— medical professional or well-meaning individual on the street—will have to throw out all their preconceived notions of what autism means, stand back, and be amazed.

If you are a parent of a child/children on the spectrum, and you've struggled with others impressions or misconceptions about your family, I am *so* sorry. Can I give you a hug? Or some chocolate at least? Just remember to please stop judging yourself. Be the best you can be in the moment. What that level is will always change, but as long as you're striving in that moment to do what is best for you and your family then you will always be the best parent you can be.

Chapter Four

What is Normal Anyway?

The world is round and I am square, and that's okay.

We live in a world afraid of labels. No one wants to be defined by one, and yet it seems there is an inherent need to place people in one box or another—to know where we each stand—in order to behave accordingly. So, when it came time to identify where my kids fit in this world, I felt guilty for needing a label. But if I could know what my kids were facing and what they were struggling with, then I could know how to help them.

In the early days, I chalked up the difficult days of being a stay-at-home mom to my own ineptitude at the task; I just wasn't a natural-born mother. Soon, I fell into a rhythm of what was normal for us. It wasn't my perfect ideal, but it worked, and we were surviving. Then I became pregnant with Colin and we'd bought our first home all in a single summer. Within a few months I was put on semi-strict bed rest with a toddler at home, a husband working full time, and no nearby family to rely on. It was so hard for me to ask for help, but I desperately needed it.

That is when my church congregation came to the rescue, in more ways than one. My husband's work was flexible enough to let him work from home in the afternoons to help with our daughter. In the mornings, neighbors would take turns watching my daughter until he came home at lunchtime. Other families brought in meals twice a week, and the women's organization even enlisted volunteers to come clean our home once a week. To this day, I firmly believe that Colin owes his survival to the members of our church.

At thirty-seven weeks, the amniotic sac fluid was tested to see if his lungs were developed enough for a safe delivery. When the test came back negative, I laid on the gurney in a ball (as much as a nine-month pregnant woman is capable of) and bawled. The kind maternity nurse silently closed the curtain around my husband and I and walked away. Tears streaked the gurney, my husband's shirt, and my face. I could not stop crying. I wanted this baby out of me. I wanted to know he was safe. And I wanted to be back on my feet taking care of my family instead of having our congregation take care of me. Four months was beyond my limit.

But I survived another three weeks of pregnancy and many more times of being served. The interchange of visiting family was a pleasant reprieve, but when things settled down and my husband went back to work, I was at home with two kids under two and still feeling like I didn't have a clue as to what I was doing.

Though forever my Energizer Bunny, running and exploring her world since the day she was born, my daughter had failed to start talking at the level of the other kids her age, in spite of our efforts at sign language helps and early reading programs.

Over the next ten months, we worked at home to help our older children practice their delayed skills. Then, Joseph made a surprise appearance when my doctor told me I was pregnant a good six months before I feel I would've been mentally prepared for another child. Though the timing wasn't ideal for me, I will never regret giving birth to my little man.

But as time marched on without me, and my kids grew, the evidences of sensory issues became more prominent. Rebekah started running into walls, literally and on purpose. I cringed as time and again my daughter would run full force into the back window or jump from the air intake vent next to our stair banister. And she never stopped. She hated eating and she despised sleeping, for both interfered with her discovery of the world around her. Throw in a new baby brother into the mix and a change in job for daddy, and any sense of routine and normalcy we might have gathered drifted like dandelions in the wind. It wasn't until a friend gently pointed out my daughter's inconsistent behaviors in relation to other kids at church her age that I truly began to question what was really "normal." Because, for my daughter, running into objects was "normal."

I may not be a brilliant mother, but I learned quickly to be open to word of mouth suggestions from friends; they might not always work, but they were always worth exploring. And more often than not, they saved my bacon. I went on gut instinct and my friend's recommendation and called an early intervention program that worked in-home with developmentally delayed children. My daughter was too old, having recently turned three, thus making her ineligible for the program; however, they identified that Colin was showing early warning signs of autism and set up rotations for an occupational therapist, a speech therapist, and a few other -ists for good measure.

Each week someone would come into our home like Santa Claus with a bag full of toys, sit down on the living room floor with my children and I, and teach me how to interactively play with my children. And each week, they would leave me with a to do list of homework to do with my children. Mostly, the items included ways of presenting myself in way that gave my kids a chance to invite me into their world and their imagination. Do you know how hard it is for a control freak to learn to let go? How hard it is to allow a child to determine how much time for play? It all seemed counterintuitive to my image of what a parent was and should be.

But it worked. It did help.

Rebekah was getting support through the early learning preschool, and Colin was slowly connecting with me through the at-home services. Then, a therapist dropped a bomb on me.

"Have you considered getting Joseph diagnosed?" she asked as we put colored beads in different segments of a muffin tin. "He's showing hints of autism like his brother."

I swear I must have had the deer-in-the-headlights look on my face.

Sure enough, Colin was transferred into the preschool program just about the same time Joseph started the at-home early intervention program. All three of my kids were showing signs of sensitivities, possible autism, and a few other developmental delays.

Fast forward to Joseph's third birthday—Joseph graduated to the preschool program with his brother, and my daughter was going into second grade. Due to Joseph's aggressive reaction to the change in his routine, our pediatrician recommended further evaluation through a pediatric developmental specialist. The only problem was that the specialist was often booked three to six months in advanced. Sure enough, the earliest the doctor could fit us in was November. We took it.

The examination room at the specialist's office was filled with toys, blocks, puzzles, comfy chairs for the adults, and a low to the ground examination table. Joseph was in heaven. He was allowed to play to his heart's content while the doctor interviewed me about my insights regarding my son, my pregnancy with him, and so on, all the while watching how Joseph played.

There were many behaviors that Joseph exhibited during the exam and subsequent tests that hinted at multiple diagnoses. But since he was barely three, the doctor made notes that we would have to rule them out as my son grew. Two years later, during a follow-up with the specialist, Joseph was formally diagnosed with social and communication disorders, previously known as Asperger's, developmental delays, aggressive tendencies, and a heart murmur for good measure. I was so relieved to have answers regarding Joseph's struggles that, after his first appointment, I scheduled visits for his siblings.

Rebekah had already participated in early intervention schooling and occupational therapy to help with her SPD, but we wanted to know the extent of her struggles, so that we, as her parents, could gain the tools to help her thrive. Her examination and tests not only proved that she showed aspects of SPD, but that she also had ADHD. The combination of these two diagnoses means that her body requires higher impacts to her joints and muscles to be able to receive the same sensory signals to the brain as a typical person hopping on one foot. That is why for years she had been repeatedly running at full speed into walls and doors and why she would climb up on ledges and tables to jump off. It also means that she is highly impacted by multiple sensory triggers. For example, if the air is blowing on Rebekah's arm, it may overwhelm her sensory signals so much that she cannot process anything else happening around her. If we want Rebekah to hear what we are saying or teaching, then she has to do physical exercise first in order to calm down her body's signals in order to allow her brain to focus.

And then there is Colin—the little boy that required me to be on bedrest for four-and-a half months for him to make it safely into this world. The child who takes "no" as a challenge, does not understand the concept of danger, and is more brilliant than both of his parents combined. The developmental specialist studied and watched him closely as we talked. I explained to the doctor that to Colin, the world exists solely for him to learn and to explore and that anything and anyone around him becomes a tool to help him process that information. If he wanted something on a high shelf, he would do anything that would help him to succeed in his goal—asking an adult for help was always a last resort.

After his appointment with the specialist, the doctor looked at me and said that I'd pretty much had already pegged my son's diagnosis all by myself. Like many autistic children, Colin showed increased aptitude in many areas, but when it came to communication, interactions, and daily personal care, he simply didn't see the value to him as a person. Those activities made no sense to my son. As such, Colin was considered moderate-functioning autistic.

What fascinated me more than anything was that the more the doctor watched Joseph, the more the doctor became excited. Even when we followed up with appointments for Rebekah and Colin, it became clear that the doctor's interest was piqued. In the end, the specialist told me that my kids were fascinating, because they were not clean-cut anything. They seemed to have picked and chosen which aspects of various "labeled diagnoses" that worked for them.

My mom asked me once if it bothered me to know that my children struggled with being labeled so many things. I told her that it doesn't change the way I feel about them. It doesn't change who they are, or who I am as their mother. It doesn't change the fact that I love them and will never regret giving birth to them. But it does help me to know that our struggles aren't all in my head. And it gives me a clear path to learn how to help them best.

For me, that makes the discovery, the diagnoses, and the labels all worth it.

Goofy Break - Part 1

Mommy's Lost It

Where Did I Leave My Sanity?

I came upstairs to start a bath for the kiddos when I swear I heard bagpipes playing. Oh Lordy, the angels be a comin' for me now, I think. Then I stop and sigh with relief. Never mind, it's just Pokémon Go in my back pocket.

I'm sure that everyone has moments in their life that make you think, "I'd lose my head if it weren't attached to my shoulders." As a spectrum parent (or maybe it's just because of who I am as an individual), I seem to have more than my fair share. We have no typical kids in our family, so I'm not sure if our kids just add that extra touch of chaotic flavor that increases the dosage and frequency of these moments.

For your reading pleasure, here are some of our more choice, sublime moments. Then you can decide for yourself if this is a Spectrum Mom thing or an "every parent" kind of thing. Or, in the end, you may decide that it's a special kind of crazy that only I can bring to the table.

******

That moment when you have to ask your son to stop eating your motivational posters, because you need to some motivation.

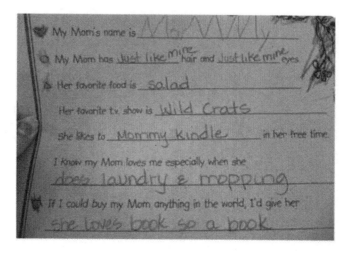

My Mom's name is Mommy

My Mom has just like mine hair and just like mine eyes

Her favorite food is salad

Her favorite tv show is Wild Crats

She likes to Mommy Kindle in her free time.

I know my Mom loves me especially when she does laundry & mopping

If I could buy my Mom anything in the world, I'd give her she loves book so a book

Figure 14 – Rebekah's 1st grade mommy survey

******

Things you should not do when on pain medication: Try to play Mario Color Splash for real.

Frank repaired holes in our stairwell by filling them with putty. Every time I went by them I was reminded of the white spots that Mario colors in with his paint hammer. So, Rebekah and I took an old sample of paint we found in the cupboard, shook it up, and decided to attempt a little real-life Mario fun. We painted in the holes.

But, instead of white spots, now we have blue. Did I mention that our stairwell is green? At least Rebekah and I have a fun memory to relive together the next time we play Mario Color Splash.

******

Experiment #2: Blowing bubbles after three Novocain injections in your mouth. You should try it.

******

While working on my computer upstairs I heard my boys breaking out in yet another fight downstairs. Exasperated I yelled back, "Please stop fighting. I'm allergic to fighting."

If only that would work.

******

I do not recommend attempting to change out a vacuum bag and cleaning out the vacuum head when wearing dress slacks and a dress shirt (especially when it's dark brown and black). I'm covered in vacuum poop. Just in time for Colin's speech therapist to arrive.

Sometimes you have to simply brush off life's poop, roll your shoulders, and tackle the next item on the *To Do* list.

******

My daughter was questioning my behavior on my medication:

Her: Mom, why do you have to take illegal drugs.

Me: They're not illegal, honey. They're prescription medications for pain, thank you very much.

Her: Oh okay, but why do they have to make you so weird?

******

Rebekah was distracted from eating her second batch of cinnamon raisin toast, so Frank took a bite of it. Turning to me, she exclaimed, "Mommy, *your* husband just ate my toast."

I replied, "I'm sorry, did you want me to do something about it?"

******

While working on a project at the library, I fiddled with my ponytail when I felt something odd. I found a fruit snack that must have been in my hair since my son wrestled me with a handful of them somewhere between lunch and dinner.

******

Never use nose spray to clean your gas permeable contacts. Crisis averted. Phew.

******

For weeks, I couldn't find the kids' bath toys. They'd just up and disappeared. Then today I finally found them. While cleaning the kitchen. They were stuffed inside my electric tea kettle.

******

Something was smelly in my living room. So, I cleaned the curtains and scrubbed everywhere, and yet when I came downstairs in the morning after a night with the swamp cooler off, there was the smell again. Then on a whim, I took out a box of baking soda and started dumping it all over the living room carpet hoping the tried and true method would solve the problem. Joseph kept trying to run under it like it was rain and laughing. Then we vacuumed it up. As I was vacuuming I noticed that when I went off the carpet into the front entrance way the tires of the vacuum left streaks. Suddenly it hit me: as I was dumping the baking soda over the carpet, the ceiling fan was on. Everything was covered in a fine layer of white powder—the couch, the desk, the shoes, the bookshelves, the couch, the toys. Still was cleaning it up the following morning. Lesson learned.

******

My kids fight a lot in May, that's how they handle the end of the school year. It's especially bad when their half-brothers go home after visiting. One time, I was in the middle of breaking up another fight and yelling "Kindness really matters!" while I was riffling through my crochet bag to see if I stuck the Kindle in there when all of a sudden, I'm like, "Ooh chocolate!" Can we say mommy squirrel moment? I had stashed a bar of dark chocolate with a caramel center and suddenly I was totally like; "I've got chocolate. What? Oh, my kids are still fighting? That's nice."

Sometimes you need a little chocolate to put life in perspective.

******

Sweet Mother of Marigolds!!! The beauty of silence that only comes when all your kids are away at school. I will now engage in the enjoyment of said silence for the next 170 minutes with utter delight so that I may love my children all the better when they return.

******

Section Two:

Mother's Truths

Chapter Five

Phone Follies

My cell phone has been missing since Friday night. I finally found it this morning when I went to change the kids' sheets. It was hidden under Colin's mattress.

When my mother was Rebekah's age, she didn't have contact with her grandparents so as Frank and I started having kids, my mom wanted to talk with our kids often. She wanted them to know that she was thinking about them, that it mattered to her what happened in their lives, and that she loved them. With impressive tenacity, my mother (or Grammy as my kids call her) has made the effort to talk to each of the kids since the day they were born. It is a sweet and lovely sentiment, with several hiccups in the works.

The first being that when Rebekah was born, we lived ten minutes away from my parents. Three months later we moved several states away—we wanted to be closer to Frank's kids from his first marriage so that Rebekah might get to know her older brothers better.

Have you ever played the telephone game?

Kids gather in a line or circle, and then one child whispers a message into the ear of the person standing next to him or her. That child then turns and whispers the message into the ears of the next kid, and so on. Once the last child has heard the message he or she announces to the group the message in its entirety.

Often a phrase like, "The kitten crossed the road" turns into, "A turkey killed the crow" until the end when the final kid loudly pronounces, "King Tut lives down the road."

This is the type of game kids learn when adults are trying to kill time during a group activity at church or school or when adults want to teach children the importance of clear communication or why gossiping about others is bad.

Now imagine playing that same game while fifty people are blowing hot air in your face, three others are pulling band-aids off of your arms one hair follicle at a time, and the vacuum is running. In the end, you'd be lucky to get a single syllable of the original message correct, let along an entire word. You can forget understanding even the gist of the conversation to begin with.

That is what it is like having a conversation with my daughter in person when she is in sensory overload.

Could you imagine attempting to have that same conversation with her over the phone?

My mother can.

When too many of Rebekah's senses are triggered at once, her brain cannot cope with the onslaught of signals and shuts down. Throw in a well-intended Grammy trying to find out how my daughter's day went, and silence reigns on the other end of the line. When Rebekah was a baby, it was understandable when she didn't respond to Grammy; she hadn't learned to speak yet. But as Rebekah got older, my mother was hoping for an equal interchange. Instead she struggled with ADHD and SPD. Frank and I realized that our daughter was zoning out on most of the conversations and wasn't processing what Grammy was asking. To Rebekah, Grammy was a disembodied voice over the thing she held in her hand, which was competing with every other sight, sound, and smell already claiming her attention in person.

Figure 15 - Rebekah talking to Grammy at five years old

Every day Grammy would call and ask our kids about what they had learned or were doing only to hear heavy breathing sprinkled with a random word or two in response. When I'd take the phone out of my kids' limp hands to talk to my mother, she'd ask if the kids were mad at her or if she'd offended them in any way.

The simple answer: no.

Being in a different time zone and state, my poor mother couldn't know that Rebekah had just come home from a hard day at school and needed time to reset herself before words would make sense. She couldn't know that Colin's mind was fully occupied as he lined up his Hot Wheels in a row all the way from the living room, up the stairs, and into his bedroom. There was no way for her to know that Joseph was recovering from a fight with his brother where one or the other ended up scratched and bleeding, sending his senses into hyper drive and making it difficult to separate the sound of Grammy's voice out of the chaos surrounding him. There was no way for my mother to realize that the hum of the swamp cooler or the kiss of its air on my daughter's skin would make it impossible for her brain to translate the signals that Rebekah's ears were registering when Grammy was speaking.

I know that my mother would love to be near her grandkids, to help them through their struggles, and to lighten my load. I know she loves them with all her heart. And I know that life, for now, means that we live in different states. In spite of not being able to observe and fully understand the obstacles my kids face on a minute by minute basis, there is something else that I know about my mother: Grammy will never give up on my kids.

Chapter Six

Water Works

My children surviving me being their mother will always be my greatest accomplishment.

Water has been both friend and foe to the Pellett household. Every summer I purchase a cheap plastic pool that I inflate with our vacuum and fill with water for hours of entertainment.

Figure 16 – Joseph - Summer 2016

However, our kids have different concepts of entertainment involving water than I do. I've seen them jump in the pool fully clothed, especially when they're in their pajamas. I've found them floating in the water, our Kindles or phones taking a bath in six inches of water by their sides. (We regularly have Ziploc bags filled with rice sitting on our kitchen counter, hoping to resurrect the abused electronics.) Other times I have found Colin dragging the toddler slide into the pool so that he could ride it headfirst into a pool already filled with Hot Wheels and Octonaut toys.

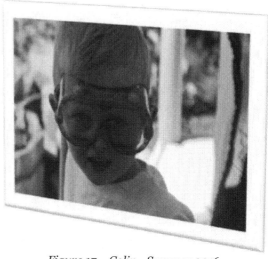

Figure 17 – Colin - Summer 2016

On days when the pool has either been pierced by fondue forks or was so torn up we had to send it to pool heaven, we've resorted to an old water table Rebekah received for her third birthday. One night, I had a "clever" idea that I continue to smack my head over. My boys were playing in the water table out back. It was a week filled with me picking my battles, so baths had been skipped from time to time. So, I devised a bath game. I brought out the shampoo and started giving them baths in the water table.

Figure 18 - Rebekah in water table - 2015

Rebekah was so enamored with the idea she ran upstairs and got her swimsuit on and came out for a "bath" as well. Things were going well until I was drying off one of the boys inside, and I heard Rebekah scream, followed swiftly by her running inside with tears streaming down her face. When I could calm her down, I finally deciphered what had happened. Mimicking her brothers, Rebekah had stood in the table. But my daughter was seven at the time and taller than the boys, so when she did a dance, she lost her balance and fell on her back on the cement.

Having done something similar when I was a kid—my having an accident involving a game of tag and a jacuzzi—I cringed. I then kissed everywhere she pointed, gave her Tylenol and an ice pack, and got her dressed for bed. After several days of close monitoring and seeing no further damage to her back, I finally breathed. I also got rid of the water table and stuck to the tried and true method of washing my little octopi in the bathtub.

Even though we love playtime in the pool, when it comes to nature's shower—rain—our family has mixed reviews. I adore the rain. I grew up in Arizona where summer monsoons were my cotton candy—sweet and sticky. The soul-crushing heat of 120 degree days made playing outside a risk for sunburns to rival a lobster's shell. We did not have a pool, and I was highly susceptible to heat stroke.

But when mid-July would approach, and the dark clouds rolled onto the mesa I would become giddy. I could feel the dampness building in the air on my skin. And, to this day, that first hint of moist dust on the wind brings back memories of me as a kid dancing in a torrent of warm rain.

Many children on the spectrum have issues with the rain (including refusing to even go outside if it is raining). I am pleased to say that my kids have inherited my love of playing in the rain. Unfortunately, with their growing sensory issues, it also brings a series of difficulties. On days when it is sprinkling and we're waiting outside for their various rides to school, my children love to stand with their heads titled back, and let the water drip into their mouths. And puddles should beware. If we're near a puddle—that world-wide children magnet—my kids run like a professional long jumper and pound on the unsuspecting pool of gathering water, splashing until they are soaked to the armpits.

And that is usually when their buses or carpools arrive to pick them up.

But, my kids can't handle staying in wet clothes. It doesn't matter if their rides are here and it is time to go. The feeling of wet cloth clinging to their bodies sends them into sensory surplus the moment they stop to breath and think. Once the overload kicks in, they are incapable of moving forward until the problem is rectified.

In the past, we've tried umbrellas as a deterrent from my kids becoming rain-soaked. But umbrellas also break faster than double stuffed OREOS disappear in our house. Rebekah loves to open her umbrella and dance, quickly becoming unaware of her surroundings (i.e. people's heads, cars, curbs, and so on). Colin prefers to throw the umbrella in the air while running away so that it makes a clunk sound as it impacts the earth. If that doesn't suit him at the time, then he'll lay it on the ground in the wrong side up and opened position to collect the precious liquid. Once enough water has pulled on the upturned shell he'll bend down and drink the rain. Whereas, my little Joseph, depending on his mood, prefers to either confiscate everyone else's umbrellas for the greater good (him) or hide under the umbrella so that he doesn't get wet at all.

So, whether they get their kicks via pools, baths, or rain my kids revel in water. But, as soon as they have moved on, this mommy must be prepared with a towel, dry clothes, a bag of rice (for our poor electronics), and a warm hug no matter whose honking their horns outside.

Chapter Seven

I Have What?

I kissed my Joseph as I walked out the door to go on a walk. Just as I reached the gate, he came running out after me and yelled, 'Hey Mom! Watch out for buffalo!' I tried. I looked all over, but not a single buffalo in sight. I'm more than slightly disappointed.

My three year old threw a car seat at my head: Joseph was three, and I had messed up his routine.

Spectrum parents will understand and nod knowingly. For all other parents, let me explain—autistic kids thrive on consistency. Mess with the familiar or their day-to-day routine, and it becomes near impossible for them to adjust or cope.

Imagine a sudden whirlwind trip to see extended family for a funeral four hours away. With little notice, we packed our bags, loaded three kids, all five and under and none of them potty-trained. Less than twenty-four hours later, we turned around to come home and got stuck in a traffic jam for six hours. Let's just say that I will never take a road trip with kids again without a portable potty stashed in my trunk.

When our beleaguered family stumbled back home, weary, smelly, and more than a bit testy, I felt like we had run a marathon. After a belated birthday dinner for our son, complete with a sad attempt at Pinterest-inspired minion cupcakes, I removed myself to the living room with Lysol wipes in hand to clean up the remnants of our eventful journey on my kids' pee-stained car seats.

Having been cooped up way too long in an automotive cell, Joseph's little mop of brown hair followed on my heels, eager to keep his safe-zone (aka mommy) within arms' reach. While I sat on the floor plucking the fabric pads off three seats, Joseph used the couch as a makeshift springboard, he bounced higher and higher, screaming, "Watch me, Mommy!"

I was tired. I was sore. And I needed a week's worth of naps, and maybe just as much chocolate. Besides, I'm afraid I had misplaced my Olympic score cards two hours earlier and was not in the mood to rate my son's jumping ability at that moment. With herculean strength, my little three-year-old lifted up his sister's car-seat and threw it in frustration. The only problem was that my head was in the way.

Whack!

Tweety birds danced around me to the beat of Beethoven's Fifth Symphony as fireworks sparkled across my vision.

The doctors confirmed what Beethoven and I already knew: I had a concussion. But just to make sure, they sent me packing off to the emergency room for an MRI. Have I mentioned that I'm claustrophobic? Have *you* seen an MRI? It's a glorified toilet paper roll made of wires and beepy things that go bump in the night. And they wanted to stuff me inside like creme in an eclair, when I already had a migraine that had me in tears and on the verge of vomiting all over the techs' pristine white Nikes. No thank you.

When the tech asked me if I was claustrophobic, I replied, "Yes."

She asked, "Have you taken something for it?"

I shook my head. "I'm not allowed." (Because, like any sane person with the lingering effects of a concussion, I drove myself to the MRI, and you aren't supposed to take anxiety meds if you are driving or operating machinery, and of course, I obey the warnings.)

She looked down at her clipboard before looking back at me. "And you still doing this anyway?"

"Yes. Yes, I am," I said, my mock bravado in full force.

Looking dubious, she replied, "Well, okay."

I bit back a retort and let her slide me into the monstrosity, scanned the insides of my brain, and prayed that the results wouldn't come back all bats in the belfry empty. I kept my eyes shut tight, reciting every lullaby I'd ever sung to my children as the tech inched me back and forth in the machine trying to find that MRI sweet spot. Soon the pounding of fifty percussion sections tapped out every John Phillip Sousa march at once within my confined space, with periodic interruptions from their conductor (the MRI tech) to fine tune their beat.

When I escaped the metallic womb an hour later, I could barely stand and I'm pretty sure my heartbeat lapped the Sousa marching band by two entire football games. It was almost a relief when the tech told me to get dressed and go home, promising a follow up call from my doctor as soon as possible.

After a week of donning sunglasses and earplugs (the only reason I didn't add a hat to this celebrity ensemble is that I'm sure the pressure of the fabric on my scalp would have irreparably damaged my sunny personality) I received a call from the doctor's office. I grabbed the phone and limped into my bedroom, closing and locking the door behind me.

"Um, we received your MRI results, and, well, we'd like to refer you to a specialist regarding your concussion." The nurse on the other end of line sounded as if she might be contemplating a change in careers right about then.

"Okay, why?" I asked, nearly missing the edge of the bed as I went to sit down.

"Well, you see, you have white matter brain lesions in atypical MS locations."

Dead silence for at least half a minute.

"We're going to refer you to a neurologist up in Salt Lake," the nurse continued.

Two boxes of Kleenex, a few weeks, and several panic attacks later, my husband and I arrived at the neurologist's office to be given my death sentence.

"Lesions are a sign that your brain has experienced trauma in its white matter," the neurologist began.

You mean like a car seat to the head? I thought.

"Your brain does show multiple lesions," she continued, oblivious of my internal sarcasm. "The good news is that they aren't in locations typically associated with multiple sclerosis."

I got that from the initial diagnosis, thanks.

"We don't know if they are a by-product of your chronic migraines, or if they are the *cause* of your chronic migraines."

"So, then it isn't MS?" my husband asked, holding tightly to my hand.

"Well, that's the thing. We don't know."

I swear my husband and I wore mirror-blank expressions.

"Where the lesions are, is not normally where we see signs of MS, but that doesn't mean it isn't possible it could be a rare form of MS."

So basically, I'm brain damaged. We do not from what. We don't know who to blame. Or if any one thing is to blame. All we know is it is there, that I need to learn to live with it, and I must be monitored for the rest of my life to make sure that the lesions don't change or expand.

It sounds mysteriously like the brain cloud that Tom Hank's character faced in the move *Joe Versus the Volcano*. In other words, like Joe, I have been given a choice: Live each day to the fullest as best I can, or blockade myself in a cave and consign myself to await the end.

Are you kidding me? Have you seen my kids? Forget the cave. Heck, forget the volcano. Forgive me while I go put on my pink wig and purple tights. I'm going trick or treating with my daughter, dressed as Twilight Sparkles from *My Little Pony: Equestria Girls*.

Chapter Eight

My Children Saved Me

The second most beautiful sound is rain fall. The most beautiful? The sound of my daughter's first cry after I went through six years of infertility, miscarriages and a high-risk pregnancy ending in a semi-emergency C-section due to preeclampsia and my daughter turning breech.

After Joseph was born, I went through a season of postpartum depression. A weight the size of Mount Olympus pressed down on me. I was so grateful to have my kids, my miracles, in my life, but man were they hard. Three kids under the age of four were daunting. Add to that the knowledge that if I ever did get pregnant again, it would most likely cost me my life. I had to choose—have my tubes tied so that I may love what I had, or risk dying and leaving my husband to raise our children as a single parent. The cost was too great in my heart, so I chose the first.

During Joseph's delivery via C-section, the doctors performed the tubal ligation. Seeing my son's face and knowing he was safely here after a rough pregnancy, I knew I had made the right decision. But there were complications. An hour into recovery, I was rushed back in for a second surgery, as blood was literally spurting out of the incision and all over the sweet nurse who was changing my dressings. I hadn't even had the chance to hold my baby yet.

I had already eaten crackers in recovery, so the medical staff was unable to sedate me for the surgery. Cranking my head to the side, I watched my husband holding our newborn son as the nurses rushed me away. My heart hurt, my soul ached, and I was scared. More scared than I had ever been. I don't know if it was premonition or just prenatal fear, but before I went into the hospital to deliver Joseph, I had written each of my family letters telling them that I love them and will always love them, even if I was no longer near. And here I was being rushed on a bumpy gurney down the chilly hallways, not knowing if I was going to survive (I have a highly active imagination. I'm really great at preparing for the worst).

For the duration of the surgery I was wide awake, praying that the fast deteriorating spinal block would last until the surgeons were finished. Praying that I would see my son again and get to know him. Praying that I would see Rebekah and Colin once more.

The doctors were able to fix the leak and sew me up. Unfortunately, I felt the last several minutes of the surgery quite clearly. But I was so fragile that I was ready to crack. In fact, I did.

The toll on my body from three high-risk pregnancies in under four years and knowing I'd never have that second girl I always wanted was more than I could physically or emotionally handle. I spiraled into depression.

It wasn't until Christmas time a year later, when my exasperated husband blurted out, "You need help," that it truly sunk in. At first, I was appalled at his bluntness and his timing, but once I'd let go of the anger, I knew he was right. The next week I made an appointment with our family doctor. His solution involved increased physical activity and antidepressant medication.

Now, I need to preface this next bit: I know that the right antidepressant for the right person can do miracles and bring back a loved one from the verge of suicide. My dear Frank knew I was depressed, because he'd seen the signs for himself in the past, and even since Joseph was born. I have friends and family members who suffer from debilitating illnesses that send them spiraling into a darkness so deep there are no shadows, because there is no light. The reason many of my loved ones even function and survive on a daily basis is through counseling and careful monitoring of antidepressant medication. And I am grateful that medication and help is there, because otherwise I might not have these dear souls with me. Having said that, I have the cursed luck of taking medication and getting all the side effects without experiencing any of the benefits.

For well over six months our doctor went through the list of antidepressant options attempting to find the right medication and dosage for me. During that time, I forgot the words to children's songs that I'd sung to my daughter every night since the day she was born. I placed child safety locks on the kids' bedroom windows, but instead of preventing the children from opening the windows, the locks were set to keep them from ever closing. Then there were the hallucinations. Once, after a rare nap, I awoke to my bedroom submerged underwater. My husband's alarm clock was a glowing red ball floating in the tide, and I watched as a mermaid and a sea dragon swam overhead.

Another time, while showering, I was transported into a massive cavern where I was flying over the remains of fossilized dinosaur bones. What scared me the most is that I was not surprised or startled by any of this. I felt like Spock from *Star Trek* when he says, "Fascinating." In fact, only once I was on antidepressants did the story of *Alice in Wonderland* ever start making sense to me.

Twice I was so dizzy from the medication that I lost my balance on the stairs and tumbled down to the first floor. Both times I carried one child or another in my arms. Shielding them from harm, I took the brunt of the damage, only stopping after plummeting into the metal security gate at the bottom of the stairs with such force it came clean off and shot across the dining room only to have me land on it. My children were uninjured, but I was not. Even more earlobes sported bruising.

After that I asked my doctor to take me off the medication. For me, they were more a hazard than a help. He agreed. And though I quickly recovered my wits once off the medication, the damage of the side effects had already taken its toll.

Between the falls and the wear and tear on my body from the pregnancies, I ruptured a disc in my back a few weeks later from getting out of the rocking chair to put my toddler back in his crib after a nightmare. The debris from the shattered disc cascaded down my back, compressing my spine until I started losing all feeling in my right leg. By the end of spring 2012, I went in for back surgery to repair the damage. Five years later, full feeling in my leg is only now returning.

During the time on the medications, I also went through a series of debilitating panic attacks. One evening, I was home alone with all three kids at the end of a stressful day balancing the needs of a four-year-old, a two-year-old, and a baby. My husband participates as part of the community band and was away for the evening preparing for a concert. The children were successfully dressed in pajamas and I was herding them up the stairs when my mother called to see how I was doing. I quickly placed Joseph in his crib and tucked Colin in his toddler bed before engaging the child gate on their opened door. Then I went to tuck Rebekah in bed.

Exhausted I lay down on the bottom bunk in my daughter's room to continue my conversation with my mom. Rebekah was wired and climbing all over me, so I handed her the phone to talk to Grammy. After their brief conversation, the phone was tossed back at my face, before Rebekah went back to playing. My boys, ever the sleep-avoiders, were yelling at each other in their bedroom. My mother made a comment about my childhood, and I took it wrong. I had a meltdown and hung up on my mother, which I *never* do, then curled into a ball on my daughter's bed.

My body was tired and battered, and now I was sobbing so hard my entire body shook and my asthma kicked in. I couldn't breathe. A full-on panic attack set in.

I can't breathe. I can't breathe.

I stumbled out into the hallway unsure of what to do. Rebekah followed me, suddenly silent, her eyes wide with fear.

Turbulent thoughts raced through my mind. *Not now. Frank's not home. What about the kids? How do I stop?*

But I couldn't stop.

I leaped over the second gate on the door to our master bedroom, ran into the bathroom, and shut the door. Slumping against the far wall, I slid down and pulled my knees up to my chin. And I rocked, chanting in my mind, *Breathe. Just breathe.*

But I couldn't.

The door to my bathroom creaked open and a tiny mop of brown curls peered around the corner.

"Mommy, what do I do?" Rebekah asked. My daughter had climbed over the fence to see if she could help mommy.

Between hyperventilating breathes I stuttered, "Pray . . .sing . . .to . . . me."

My little four-year-old took me by the hand and led me from the bathroom into my bedroom. Sitting me on the floor, she crawled onto my lap. Folding her arms, and closing her eyes, she prayed. "Dear God. Help mommy to breathe. And help daddy to come home soon."

Tears spilled down my cheeks onto her head. I pulled her in tightly. "Thank . . .you."

Rebekah drew on my arms around her tiny body into a hug, then tucking her head under my chin, she began to sing. Her voice was soft, sweet, pure, and healing. She sang through the list of songs I would sing to her every night before bed, all the time keeping my arms wrapped around her.

Then Colin, who does not see the point of communication and who had been watching from his bedroom began to sing along with his sister. And Joseph calmed down, sitting quietly in his crib, listened intently. The vice on my lungs loosened, and my sobbing waned. After the last strains of *Summertime* faded, I took my first deep breath in over an hour. Hugging Rebekah tightly I inhaled in, savoring the smell of her freshly washed hair, and whispered, "Thank you."

When Frank returned from band practice, he found me sitting on the floor of Colin and Joseph's room with all three children piled on my lap as we read story after story from their bookshelf.

Now when I face a day that is especially hard I pull my daughter close and ask, "Rebekah, can you sing to me please?" And as I hold her close and listen to her sweet voice, I look at my three children and remember the day they saved me.

Goofy Break - Part 2

Really?

Are You Kidding Me Moments

I love making my daughter laugh, simply to see her eyes sparkle.

Every family has those moment when you shake your head and wonder if anyone else is as crazy as yours. If you don't, then here are some of our Pellett family moments that will leave you either smiling or shaking your head. Your choice. Because in our home, laughter is truly one of the best medicines.

******

Rebekah charged into the living room with a scream and waved the new Swiffer duster in the air like a sword. With her eyes gleaming she ran up to me and gave me a hug. "I love my new weapon."

"Oh, yeah?" I asked, squeezing her back. "What's it for?"

"Getting rid of ghosts," she replied. Then she ran back upstairs to finish fighting the demons of the universe before dinner time.

******

Colin was having a meltdown outside our room when I heard him yell, "Ow, ow, ow!"

I asked him, "Are you okay?"

"No!" He replied. "I need Kindle."

Nice try little man, but that is not how you get your way.

******

Newest Rebekah-ism —Frank and Rebekah were making cookies in the kitchen, when I heard Frank telling Rebekah not to eat raw dough because of the uncooked eggs. Two minutes later my daughter comes running into the living room licking the beater and saying, "Hey mom, look at me. I get to eat rotten eggs."

My husband tried to clarify the difference between rotten eggs and raw eggs, but Rebekah just cracked a joke back at him.

Finally, he tells her, "You're silly."

Rebekah laughed and replied, "Yes, I am."

******

In the fall, I spent two hours pulling up plants and cleaning up the garden/backyard for winter. Then I went to the library to work on an editing project for a friend. When I returned several hours later, Joseph was trying to ride his bike in the raised garden bed like a BMX rider.

******

Frank and I finally introduced our children to *Herbie Goes Bananas*. When we got to the part where the cruise captain sends Herbie overboard, poor Rebekah kept asking "Is Herbie going to die? I bet he's going to die. Just tell me. Is he dead?" This went on for about ten minutes.

******

My autistic son had been doing experiments with soap and water in his bedroom for three days in a row and now both of our Kindles are in bags of rice. We do a lot of praying around here that the Kindles (and my sanity) might be saved.

******

Apparently "quiet time" at the Pellett household means jumping off your bed onto the ground to make the loudest thud you can and then laughing your head off. If that doesn't work then you hop fences and run down stairs maniacally giggling until you make mom concerned enough to find out what is happening. Or, if that doesn't work, you stand outside mom's door knocking and saying, "Hello. Is anyone there?" And if that doesn't work, you press your back against mom's door and push with your feet in a vain attempt to force her door open.

******

When Joseph doesn't want me on my laptop, he'll come running up and slam the lid down on my fingers. I tried putting my foot out to block him from doing that. But now he thinks it's the most hilarious thing to run purposely into my foot hard enough with his chest to fall backwards on his butt. Hey, whatever makes him happy.

******

I tried to lay on the floor to do back stretches since my back was wigging out on me (back surgery can do that to a person). I propped my legs up on the couch and was getting ready to lift my butt in the air for a bridge bend when Colin jumped on my legs, flopped on my belly, and landed on my head. The boys then preceded to use my entire body (including my head and shoulders) as I trampoline. It felt like I've been attacked by a hoard of angry snapping turtles (And might need traction for a week to recover).

******

Colin propped the exercise trampoline against the couch, slid down it and said, "Oh my gosh!" And then repeated the same routine for the next hour.

******

Reminder to self: never perch your leg over the arm rest when sitting in a recliner. When this happens, your kids will see it as a trampoline or spring board and jump onto your foot from the couch armrest. Ouch! And they will try to repeat.

******

Can someone please create waterproof electronic devices for kids? What's the point of getting them a tablet or any learning tool when they're going to love it so much that they take it into the bathtub with them?

******

Colin thinks the best toy ever is the toilet plunger. He keeps sticking it onto his belly and walking around shaking it side to side and then jumping up and down on the couch to see if it stays on. I can't stop laughing.

******

Colin moved the exercise trampoline into the kitchen to see if he could bounce high enough to get to the Halloween candy. This is especially funny since he doesn't usually eat sweets.

******

Just before lunch I heard Joseph playing with the washer and dryer while I was sitting in the living room. Usually he likes to put a car in the empty machine and then rotate the drum in a circle to see if the car will ride along or fall with a clang to the bottom. When I got up to make lunch, I realized I still heard the sound, but Joseph wasn't standing by the laundry closet, and both machines were closed. Then I hear a "Hi, Mom!" I looked around but didn't see him. Then he said, "Down here." I looked down through the front door of the dryer and realized he was sitting inside the dryer, playing with the door closed and waving at me.

******

Putting a positive spin on things:

1) I went to tuck my kids into bed and almost stepped on the inside latch to a door knob. At first I thought it was one of the old ones that I had replaced last week and that Colin had found it on the dryer and had gotten it down to play with. Nope—my five-year-old removed his own door knob off of the door, which is pretty ingenious since he'd only ever watched me work on the other knobs.

2) Then he handed me one of the hooks that he'd ripped out of the wall the other night when he yanked out the pet net. Instead of getting frustrated again, I took a deep breath and said, "Thank you for handing this to me. I'd hate to have stepped on it." Colin said, "You're Welcome!" Dude, that's huge. This is my autistic son, who doesn't understand the point to communication. He actually said something in words in response to my comment, and it was clear, concise, and completely beautiful. (I'm glad that I took that deep breath.)

What is the positive spin? you ask. His bus driver called the same day to confirm the time and location for picking Colin up for school. Only one week until this momma can breathe a little easier.

******

My sweet, brilliant, tenacious, autistic son discovered I had changed the locks on our bedroom door. He went downstairs, got his father's keys, found a key that would fit, and made it work, thus letting himself into our bedroom. Then he went into the closet and tore apart Frank's tools, dumping them all on the floor, taking apart everything he could, and tossing everything in a big heap. Then he went into his sister's room, moved the dresser that was blocking her closet, opened the closet door, moved the dresser back, climbed on the dresser to get up to the higher shelves, knocked down the VHS tapes and other bags hidden in there, pulled down the airbed and tossed it on the floor, took down the chest of Legos that Frank had hidden on the uppermost shelf, and pulled them down and dumped them out on the floor. He then played with them quietly while the rest of the family was downstairs watching a movie.

Game on.

******

The boys got into the Halloween makeup and spilled it all over the carpet on the stairs and their faces. They then sprinkled sparkles everywhere as they danced around the house.

******

Colin took the Swiffer duster and hit the TV with it and cracked the plasma. Then not ten minutes later, my cell phone fell out of my pocket and cracked on the tile. Who knew Halloween was going to be so nightmarish?

******

My daughter is playing with an app on the Kindle that has cats playing jazz. She said, "It sounds SOOO much better with the upright bass, but cats playing jazz . . .that's SOOOO fiction!"

******

Dangers of potty training boys:
1. Missing the toilet.
2. Peeing all over mommy's brand new replacement phone.

******

Trying to watch Hulu as a family, and it keeps shutting off. In hope of teaching my children to use words instead of tantrums I said, "Oh, that is so frustrating."

My Colin cried out in his own frustration, "Oh, my chinny chin chin."

I like his response better.

******

Joseph is attempting to close himself inside the fridge.

******

We're watching the Muppets movie, and when Kermit and Fozzie try to get Gonzo to join the team, Gonzo is standing on top of his company building when he takes off his clothes and says he's been wearing his cape under his suit for years. Then pushes a self-destruct button on his business and then jumps.

Colin ripped off his clothes and did a summersault off the armrest and on to the couch.

Yep, that's my life.

******

I started singing, "Ooh ooh ooh ooh," and all three kids chimed in with, "Staying alive. Staying alive." And they all started dancing. Talk about proud parenting moment.

******

About two weeks ago, Colin figured out how to open the fridge. Today he figured out how to open the carton of eggs, throw one of the floor, crack it open and play with the goo inside and then lick his fingers. The kid is a quick learner.

Figure 19 - Colin investigating eggs at two years old

******

I just found an opened box of mac 'n cheese in the kids' bedroom, and Colin had been eating the uncooked pasta. Guess he won't be hungry for dinner then.

******

I love it when my daughter comes walking into the kitchen and sees what I'm making for dinner and says, "No, what are we REALLY eating for dinner?"

Section Three:

Home is a Battle Zone

Chapter Nine

Bubble Wrap, the Ultimate Distractor

I told Rebekah to give me a moment until I have a free hand. 'Since when do hands cost money?' Rebekah asked.

Rat-tat-tat. The key slides into the hole and, with just the right pressure, the tumblers rotate and the door unlocks with a click; because we *had* to install a deadbolt on the front door. To. Keep. Our kids. In.

The cool autumn breeze kisses my cheek with a hint of wood smoke. A neighbor must have started a fire in their chimney early this year. As I peer out of the gap in the door, I look around, but the stoop is empty. There, at my feet, is a package the size of a small Labrador. It's a simple cardboard box, sealed with clear packing tape. As if on cue, the pounding of footsteps echoes from above.

How do they know? *How* do they always know when a package arrives?

With a skip in my breath I slide the package inside the house, locking the deadbolt, and slipping the key back to the safety of the thumbtack, well out of reach of inquisitive hands. My daughter conquers the last four stairs with a giant leap. I cringe on impact, but Rebekah breaks into a run without a hiccup in her stride or energy.

Colin tackles the banister, climbing onto the nearby intake air vent and makes jump shots with a foam ball into the basketball net hanging from the ridge of the adjacent closet. Two seconds later, the thump-thump-thump announces Joseph as he slides head first on his belly down the stairs.

Figure 20 – Two year old Joseph unwrapping a package

My kids dance around my legs like I am a maypole as I balance the target of their excitement over my head, making a vain attempt to reach the kitchen counter. Questions overlapped questions, twisting the children's words into near-incomprehensible gibberish.

"Can I see? Can I see?" Joseph yelled over his siblings.

"What is it?" Rebekah chimed in.

Stumbling over my own feet, I reach the safety of the small kitchen in our townhome and struggle to grab a steak knife from the child-protected silverware drawer. When I can't get the safety latch loose, my autistic son does it for me. With a sigh that would do my mother proud, I took the knife in his hands and slip its serrated ridges under the edge of the box, piercing the barrier preventing my children from their ultimate prize.

Joseph grabbed the wooden dining chairs from the table and tugged them over to the kitchen counter, the tattered legs protesting with a grind against the linoleum floor. Scrambling onto the scarred surface of the counter despite my warnings, both Rebekah and Joseph crowd in, while Colin rubs his palms up and down the sides of the cardboard grail.

A cheer erupts from the little ones when the last of the packing tape breaks free from the box with a pop.

"Let me see," Rebekah shouts, lifting one flap of the lid.

"But it's my turn," Joseph yells. He elbows his sister in the ribs. She pushes him back, nearly sending him to the floor, but for a swivel of my hip that halts his fall.

I reach into the deceptive treasure chest and pull out the object of their affections: the bubble wrap.

Bouncing up and down like kangaroos on sugar, they each try to get at the plastic protective wrap first. They do not care what object the wrap is protecting. They want the prize. Using the steak knife, I slice the wrap into three equal portions and hand one to each child.

Without so much of a thank you, the kids attack the bubbled surface with epic force. Rebekah and Joseph hop down from the counter and, laying the bubble wrap on the cold linoleum, begin a full-on assault. Loud crackles of bursting plastic erupt in the air as Colin covers his ears, his tiny portion held tightly in one hand. He giggles, but the flurry of movement and sound is too much for him to handle. So he grabs the now empty box from the counter and lugs it upstairs, where he will enjoy the pleasure of applied physics (usually involving a mattress-shaped ramp and a tricycle) from the safety of his bedroom.

Figure 21 - Rebekah popping bubble wrap

In the meantime, I pull out the green foam earplugs that are always present in my pockets and silently walk through the mounting chaos into the living room. Lying down on the couch, I unwrap the throw that had arrived in the package, and grab the book I was reading before the resounding knock had changed our lives forever—or at least for the next half hour.

Chapter Ten

The Smelling Salt Debacle

My doctor once told me, "Just remember, when you get to the end of your rope, tie a knot and hang on." I'm trying lately to focus on the miracles in my life, even on the hard days. So, I've modified his saying into the following, "Just remember, when you get to the end of your rope make a swing out of it and kick back and enjoy that moment of stillness and peace as you fly."

A Spectrum Mom is required to be a household ninja.

Why?

Just ask the woman who had to monitor her son's poop to make sure he passed the foam earplugs that he swallowed. There have also been times that I've had to yank string from unmentionable places because a child was stuck on the potty after swallowing a thread he pulled off his pant leg. You learn to know where your children are at all times and to pinpoint any possible items that might be used for oral investigation. I've had to stop my kids from eating chalk, asphalt, crayons, plastic, bottle caps, and much more. Items that seem innocuous at first, but in an instant, can morph into weapons of oral destruction in the hands of a sensory investigator.

Some people say I'm a little anal in my watchfulness over my children. Maybe so. But nothing has ever terrified me more than when my autistic son returned from a father and son campout.

I grew up in a family that went camping together. It wasn't often, and it wasn't grand, but what always impressed me was that my mother, who preferred a hotel with bathroom facilities and a television, would go camping with us—actual tent pegs in the ground, in the middle of the woods, or next to a lake, camping. My parents would load my brother and I in our sometimes working, vehicle, and head north to Show Low or Payson, Arizona, where we would spend the weekend learning to fish. We rarely ever caught anything. But the memory has ingrained itself into my soul, and because of my mother's sacrifice, I have also held a love for camping, hiking, and the outdoors. Hence, I have made it my goal that one day I will have the courage to take my kids camping as well.

Have I yet? Nope. Will I eventually? I hope so.

So when my husband one day offered to take Colin on a father and son campout for church, I was cautiously optimistic. Now my husband is not what I would consider an outdoors kind of guy. He's quirky and loves playing video games, watching Japanese anime, and delving into a good book. But a camper? Not my Frank. He also has fibromyalgia, so he is in pain pretty much all day, every day. And yet he is also filled to the brim with perseverance.

Frank approached another spectrum dad at church and asked him for advice on how to best introduce your autistic son into such activities. The answer? Slow and steady wins the race. Try a little each time until they get used to it.

My husband decided to take the plunge. He took the time off work, packed their bags, a first aid kit, and a sleeping bag and hitched a ride with another congregation member up to the campsite.

They returned not four hours later.

When they'd arrived at the camp site, Colin eagerly explored the new surroundings. Frank kept to his side as much as he could, but Colin is a natural explorer and often gets lost in his surroundings, with no concept that someone might worry if he were to wander away. By dinner time, Colin had had enough investigation and was ready to go home. One problem—Frank hadn't driven. By bedtime, Colin was melting down, and they'd found a patient individual willing to bring them all the way back home. Tired and sore, they walked in the house and plunked their bags on the kitchen counter. I don't think Colin even gave me a hug as he lumbered up to bed, put his pajamas on, and fell asleep.

The campout had occurred in the middle of May, which is often a rough time in our household due to the end of the school year and the family routine changing. Needless to say, none of us cared to put away the camping supplies that lay forlorn on our counter tops.

A few days later, I was indisposed in the downstairs restroom when a child's pained cry ripped through the air. I rushed out of the bathroom as Colin ran into my arms, tears dripping down his pale face and his tongue hanging out. I wrapped him in my arms and tried to get him to tell me what happened.

When he wouldn't answer my questions, I tried sign language, but he was too upset to respond. Then, he began rubbing furiously at his tongue. On the counter lay an opened backpack, signs of it having been riffled through strung all over the counter. There, on the floor lay an abandoned first aid kit with a semi-disintegrating smelling salt beside it.

With one hand, I called Poison Control, while with the other I held my sobbing son and tried to coax fluids down his blistered throat.

The patient man on the other end of the line went silent when I explained what had happened. Finally, he stuttered, "Get him to the hospital now."

My husband watched the kids as I put Colin into his car seat and raced to the nearest hospital, despite it not being on the insurance carrier's approved list. For four hours, I sat by his bedside in the emergency room as the nurses and doctors took turns monitoring him for damage to his esophagus and making sure that he could breathe. Four hours of singing lullabies and stroking his cheek and the bridge of nose to keep him still.

Now I ask you, would you become a household ninja after an experience like that?

Chapter Eleven

Safety Zone

After several days of Joseph running a high fever, Frank told me, "Joseph's fever finally broke." Joseph came running into the kitchen sobbing and threw his arms around my legs. I asked, "What's wrong, honey?" Joseph cried, "I broke my fever."

Since they were crawling, my kids have found refuge in tight spaces. They find comfort in four walls. When it came to quiet time they would unwittingly go to their rooms, as long as I left their door open. But being the rambunctious twits that they are, they are also escape artists and constantly get into dangerous situations. Thus, began the evolution of the attempt at childproofing our townhome.

I call it an evolution as it is constantly changing as we find a greater and greater need to reinvent the meaning of safety in our home. My first attempt was to keep my daughter from closing herself into the entertainment unit by tying yarn around the door knobs, preventing her from opening one or the other cabinet doors. Rebekah had the habit of opening the doors, taking out every single DVD we owned, then crawling inside the cupboard and closing the door behind her. There she would stay for long stretches of time leaving me to run panicking around the house calling her name. That vain attempt at a solution lasted but a few weeks. She quickly learned that the string was removable.

Fine, I thought. Let her climb into the cabinets—she needs the sense of safety and comfort the tight space afforded her. Instead, we moved the DVDs to the bookshelves, but that failed to stop her from taking out all the videos and playing with them. Then we tried poster board Velcroed to the bookshelves, hiding the movies from sight. But she figured out that deterrent in a matter of days. But by then, Rebekah had moved from DVDs to the kitchen, where she found great joy in

removing all of my pots and pans from the cupboards. Once the shelves were bare, leaving me a metal maze to navigate through the kitchen to get to her, she would climb into the

Figure 22 - Rebekah sorting DVDs - 2008

kitchen cupboards, and lie down on the shelves.

By then I was pregnant with Colin, and we'd moved into our current home. Little did I know that Colin would be more than a match for all of us put together when it came to problem solving. His spatial reasoning and complex problem solving skills are Olympic in nature.

Since our townhome had stairs, we placed a metal safety gate at the bottom of the stairs and another at the top. We even equipped the kitchen cabinets with child-safety latches. Did that stop my kids? Ha! Hardly.

With two trained safety equipment assassins now at large, my kitchen cupboards would burst open with broken or loose latches before Colin was even one year old. By that time, his sister had even showed him how to avoid the complications of the gates on the stairs by climbing over the banisters and jumping from there to the living room carpet.

And what to my panic-stricken mommy soul would appear, but a third little investigator, Joseph, closing up the rear. With three kids four years and under I again tackled the problem of child safety in our home. But dear little Joseph followed swiftly in his siblings' footsteps. This time adding to the safety-alert menu the habit of climbing into the dryer and closing himself inside.

I had latches on my drawers, double latches on my lazy Susan turntable, triple latches on the oven and fridge, and yet my kids would invariably bypass the child security system or simply break them. I swear the cashiers at Home Depot knew us by name as we came through on a regular basis with a new idea of how to childproof our house. The only thing our house was proof of was that either future engineers or criminal masterminds lived there. I think our family alone kept the makers of every child safety manufacturer in business for a solid three years.

By the time Joseph was two, we started keeping the kitchen chairs on top of the counter, just to prevent the children from using them as stepping stools to climb on the counter. Then when I caught Colin using his toy box to climb on the counter and then on top of the chairs perched on the counter to get to the space above the kitchen cabinets, I was beyond frazzled. Our piano bench was on top of the piano. Our dining chairs on top of the table, pushed far away from the kitchen counter. Would I have to remove all semblance of furniture from our home just to keep my kids safe?

Once, during naptime, I even caught Colin making multiple trips downstairs by jumping over the security gate on his bedroom door, opening the one at the top of the stairs, then running down to the kitchen where he retrieved the steak knives from on top of the refrigerator. When I found him, he was laying out the steak knives in a straight line on the floor next to his sleeping baby brother. Knowing my son, I don't think it even crossed his mind the horror film image this created; he was doing what came normal to his autistic tendencies—finding cool objects and putting them in linear order.

It was about this time that I started replacing door knobs everywhere in the house. First, we moved up to simple locks with a slit on the outside of the knob which required me to insert a coin or something else flat and turn to unlock the door. After around four months, I replaced those with the style that required a chuck key to open. Six months later I began the process anew, changing out the pantry door, the master bedroom door, and the front door with locks that required keys to open.

And yet my children often found my efforts a simple challenge—a puzzle to figure out until they achieved the end goal. They have always been explorers and investigators, and they will not allow anything to stand in their way. Even mommy.

In fact, the reason we had to replace the front door deadbolt with one that required a key to unlock from the inside as well as the outside. The main reason? Colin would let himself out front and explore the neighborhood. I don't mean just looking about. He would check every single door in our complex until he would find one unlocked. Then, without knocking—let alone asking permission—he would begin exploring our neighbors' houses. And if he found something he liked, he took it. He didn't see it as stealing. In Colin's world, everything and every person exists solely to solve a puzzle. He does not understand the concept of social rules let alone that he should follow them.

One day in frustration, I yelled, "Stop breaking into the neighbors' houses."

But my dear, sweet son had already moved onto bigger and better plans.

As a solution to this problem, I do not take my kids out front to play anymore unless there are at least three adults who can keep track of where and what my kids are doing *and* what danger they are getting into. There is no such thing as safety proofing the world for my kids or from my kids. Instead we have modified the rules in our house and raised money for equipment that will allow our children to satisfy their sensory signals in the safety of our own home. We may have a tiny back yard, but it has a porch swing, a trampoline with kid proofing insulation around the bars (though Colin did tear apart the safety mat covering the springs and shredded the entirety of the foam bumpers, strewing them all across the back yard, but that's another story). We also allow the kids to jump on our couches, especially during inclement weather. Our counselor provided us with a punching bag for aggressive moments. And we have a plethora of boxes and tight spaces for our kids to hide in when they need a break from sensory overload.

As for the daggers and steak knives—I've learned not to cook with them. They are buried away deep into the hidden crevices of the house to the point I can't even find them. If I do ever need them, I'll just ask my kids. I'm sure they'll locate them in less than a week.

Chapter Twelve

I Can't Think About That

Things I thought I'd never have to say: "Please stop breaking into the neighbors' houses."

When my children were toddlers my mom would ask me, "Do you worry about the possibility of them never getting married? That they may never have children? That they may never leave home?" I heard these questions, and many extensions of them, throughout the years from all sorts of people. And I'll tell you what I learned about myself through years of being their mom (and many counseling sessions): I can't think about that right now.

"Why?"

Because my family needs me not to.

I refuse to think about the fact that my daughter may never have a truly close best friend because she is regularly bullied for being different. If I did, I'd never let her out of the house for fear of her being betrayed or hurt by those see interacts with each and every day.

I won't stress about the possibility of my son never going off to college, even though he is stinkin' brilliant. If I did, I would worry about what secondary education will be available in fifteen years for a man with moderate-functioning autism, let alone how to pay for it. I'd worry about how he would live independently enough and have the focus required to achieve such a dream. And, I'd worry if it were my dream being forced upon him because he can't tell me what he would like to do when he grows up.

I can't stress about whether or not my children will ever get married or about their future family life. If I did that, it would burst open the floodgates for a waterfall of other worries. Such as, if they don't have a family of their own, will they live the rest of their lives not knowing the joy and love of finding a companion that complements them? Will they never experience the happiness, the sorrow, and the absolute miracle of bringing children into this world? And if I focus on the possibility of my children never knowing that blessing I would never stop crying.

Thinking about my children's inability to understand danger and Colin's tendency to escape into the neighborhood to explore would nearly paralyze me. With my active imagination, I would envision a time we wouldn't be able to find him. And if I thought that I might never see my boy's beautiful, explosive smile again I would hug him and never let him go.

Then, there is the concern about what happens when my boys grow up and become taller and stronger than me? Will there be a moment they become over sensitized to the point they lash out and become a physical danger to themselves, and others? If they did, I would have to put them in a facility more capable of meeting their needs than I. Logical or not, realistic or not, I would feel that I had failed them.

What if my children's special needs make it impossible for them to ever live independently? Will I have to give up my dreams of traveling the world once I achieve "empty nester" status—to be the grandmother whose family wonders where in the world Grandma is today. And what happens to my children when my husband and I pass away?

Those are all fears that I don't have the capacity to think about today.

If I focus on all the *What if* questions in my life, then the zombie apocalypse might as well start right now, because I would move into my closet, curl into a ball, and weep until my soul ran dry.

Physically, emotionally, and mentally I do not have it in me. I already suffer from frequent migraines, fatigue, high blood pressure, and stress-induced weight gain. Why would I want to add more fear and worry on top of *that* already over-flowing plate?

I simply cannot do that. I do *not* have the time. I do *not* have the energy.

Instead I live each day *not* thinking about the things I cannot control so that I can survive and thrive in the *here* and *now*. I don't think about those questions as I wake up every morning, take a shower, and get dressed.

I set the worries aside as I gather the kids' school clothes and walk into my children's rooms singing, "Wake-y wake-y eggs and bake-y, how does your garden grow?" And if I ever stop singing early, I grin as all three of my children finish the song for me.

I don't think about the future as I help them focus on step-by-step routines: having our cereal with milk or juice on the side, getting dressed and wearing slip on shoes because my kids will most likely never be able to tie a bow, kissing the favorite stuffed bunny goodbye, but ensuring the smaller pink unicorn is safe in a backpack to help my daughter through her anxiety that day.

Instead, I take care of the laundry, the shopping, the cleaning, my volunteer hours, my writing and more while the kids are at school, so that I can give them the best focus I might have left when they return.

Then, when they are home I am more capable of helping them with their homework, dance with them to their favorite learning song, watch YouTube videos on how to create epic toy stunts, teach them how to cook/bake what little they do eat, play Mario Kart 8 with them, perform science experiments, kiss their hurts, squish each other with love, lay on the floor and kick balloons in the air with our feet, and tell them how grateful and glad I am to be their mommy.

I'm not saying that I don't ever face my list of future unknowns; they are always there in my mind's peripheral vision. But if I don't learn to live in the moment, then I would be paralyzed by fear and never be able to see just how incredible, intelligent, funny, and talented my children are right now in this moment.

And that's how I carry on each day. That's why I keep putting one foot in front of the other, and leave the future to deal with itself.

Goofy Break —Part 3

Confessions

Parental Coping Moments

Mommy Truths

You know your life is hard when you go to counseling and make your therapist cry just listening about your day.

I love my kids to the dickens and back, but they can be hard. At the end of the day I find myself often feeling the same brand of sensory overload my children experience. During those moments, I take to my journal and come up with the following nuggets of wisdom (in no particular order).

So welcome to my mommy twilight zone—that super special place in my mind where I discover elemental truths about my role as a mother. Tread carefully if you dare.

******

Tonight, at bedtime, my husband asked if I wanted to watch something or have him read to me.

My response, after the kids had spent the last hour in hyper-drive, "Can we please watch something? I need some time to reset my brain before I'll be able to cope with listening."

******

My daughter: Mom, you are so beautiful and you don't have a single wrinkle either.

Me: That is the SWEETEST, kindest, most wonderful thing to say to me right now. I LOVE YOU.

******

My husband: I know, you like to have something to stress over.

Me: No, I just like to identify any possible conflicts far in the future so that I can find solutions long before I need them.

******

Rebekah has been copying everything we say and do today. This morning when I came downstairs Frank said, "Hiya, hot stuff," and Rebekah said, "Hiya, hot stuff." This afternoon Colin was upset and I was rubbing his foot and telling him it was all okay. Rebekah grabbed Colin's other foot, started rubbing it, and said, "It's okay, Colin." Then when I patted his head and kissed it, she did the same. So cute. Now if she hadn't made him cry in the first place, that would have been even better.

******

My daughter was playing with my foot while we were having a conversation about women's rights to vote. I'm to the point that I can't think and talk at the same time and her rubbing my foot was sending me into sensory overload.

I yelled, "Stop rubbing my vote!"

******

The beauty of school is that it helps me to actually be appreciative of my kids when they get home. I get distance and perspective and the kids get a break from their mom. It's a win/win in my book.

******

Never run in a Darth Vader boot/walking cast after an escaping Joseph while waiting for the school bus. It's just not fun, so don't do it.

******

Man, I get one short, glorious nap (and my husband isn't even working from home today), and all of a sudden, I'm like, "Let's watch *Animaniacs!*"

I can't imagine what it will be like when Joseph starts school, and I could get a nap every morning if I wanted. When they get home, I might be all, "Let's paint splotches on the ceiling, smoosh our hands in pudding, and do handstands until we pass out."

Wow, how a little break and some rest can change how you handle life.

******

While I was cleaning the carpet downstairs, one of the children who had refused to poop all day finally let loose and then walked through it all in our bedroom. Thanks to him I cleaned our bedroom carpet as well.

Said kid was so grossed out by the experience that we're hoping he has seen the benefit of learning to go in the potty. But hey, thanks for the extra workout.

******

I have come to the conclusion that teaching children how to play board games is not my forte. It only ends up in wailing and gnashing of teeth—and that's just on my part. Why did they have to start with *Clue?* Couldn't they have picked something easier like, I don't know, pixy sticks or something.

******

Oh, my gosh! We are watching *Lilo and Stitch* and I'm dying laughing. Suddenly, Lilo and Nani's personalities and actions feel like somebody has been secretly watching our family and taking notes. The randomness of their conversations and reactions to situations especially hit home.

******

I took the kids outside in the front yard all by myself for the first time since October-ish. This is freakin' HUGE people!!!! Now don't mind me while I go ice my knee and take a nap to recover from two hours of kite flying/bubble blowing/Frisbee tossing/chalk drawing/scooter fun.

******

Dear *Little Einstein's* Creators:

When you use the same piece of classical music for two different episodes my kids will notice and it confuses the heck out of them. Please stop.

Thanks,

A Mom of Smarty Pants Kids

******

I was so overwhelmed by multiple things yesterday that I went into sensory overload (instead of my kids doing it). It was so bad that I went to the fridge and got out the leftover chocolate mousse frosting from a cupcake order I'd completed and took out a package of Oreos. Then in all gloriously stressed out fashion I dipped the Oreos directly into the mousse and indulged in decadent chocolatey goodness. Seriously, who needs the cupcake base when you have an Oreo for an edible spoon and the mousse tastes like the sumptuous innards of a French silk pie without the pie crust.

******

Finished my three day at-home sleep test and only got five and a half to six and a half hours total combined of sleep each night. I jokingly said to the sleep study lady on the phone, "No wonder I'm so tired." She asked, "Do you take naps during the day?" I told her, "No, but I have three little kids at home." She said, "That would do it."

******

Random Thought #3—You know you are a parent when you've tried everything else and finally look at your child, tilt your head, and say, "Do you REALLY want me to react to that? 'Cause if you REALLY want me to react, then I will react. But are you sure?"

And then they stop what they are doing and have to think about whether or not they actually want you to react or not.

******

I'm attempting to teach my children the importance of respect, kindness, and the power of listening to others while teetering on the brink of matching my children meltdown for meltdown. Oh, heaven help me, I'm being overrun by mini-mes.

******

In the last four days, I've changed a shower head (with one minor addition of plumber's tape from the husband before he left), repaired a banister, moved the rubber stoppers on our child safety gate to better fit the replacement gate, hung a curtain rod over the kitchen window, repaired some damage to the garden (thanks to the kids), mowed the backyard using a weed whacker, weeded the garden beds, gotten all three kids haircuts, touched up my own roots, and replaced my social security card. Now I'm cutting out fabric squares that I've had lying around the house to finally start a quilt for my daughter that I planned three years ago. And tomorrow I get to fix the living room curtain rods, thanks to kids that think curtains are for swinging on like little monkeys.

Watch out world—this woman is on a mission and is wielding power tools and ambition.

******

I'm grateful for inside jokes.

I'm grateful for migraine meds.

I'm grateful for patient teachers.

I'm grateful for long showers.

I'm grateful that my house is still standing and that our cars still relatively work.

I'm grateful for an amazing husband who thinks one day I'll make enough money on writing to buy a bigger house on my paycheck alone (now that's either faith or sweet delusion—I'll take either one).

I'm grateful for friends who laugh at my stories in all the right places, then help me make it even better.

I'm grateful for surviving two sets of doctor visits with all three children in tow and that no one has anything worse than the common cold.

I'm grateful for peanut butter M&Ms and Dr. Pepper at our writers group.

I'm grateful for books borrowed from friends because the wait time at the library is way too long.

I'm grateful for inspiration.

I'm grateful for prayer.

And I'm still grateful for dark chocolate.

******

I was lying in bed working on my laptop when I read a post from an editor about something not to do when submitting a manuscript. I showed my husband and then said, "I should go back and make sure I've never done something like that."

Frank got all animated and pointed at the television. "When did you ever shoot fish with a gun, honey?"

That's what I get for catching up on Facebook while watching *Mummy: Tomb of the Dragon Emperor* while my husband is trying to read a book. Sometimes our mixed conversations when we're both out of whack and tired are quite the roller coaster.

******

This afternoon I was struggling with one of the chapters I was writing, and I yelled out to no one in particular, "How do I write a vision quest?" And Rebekah yelled back, "You start with 'help wanted.'"

******

I just *adore* the sound of Joseph's laughter. It is very complex and has different levels. There is the Ernie from *Sesame Street* level, then there is the Cookie Monster laugh, then comes the full-body-you're-so-funny-I-just-have-to-fall-over-I'm-laughing-so-hard. And when that laugh comes out, the two cutest, little dimples in the whole world grace his cherub cheeks. Yep he's a corker and a keeper.

******

Today is one of those days that when I discovered a Fruit Loop on the living room floor by the Christmas tree I ate it because it was easier than walking all the way into the kitchen to throw it in the trash. When I realized what I had done I simply shrugged and counted it as my morning snack.

******

Figure 23 - Rebekah's Mother's Day drawing of me

Section Four:

Hard Lessons

Chapter Thirteen

Outside Help

I made the pharmacist laugh the other day. When I was picking up my anxiety meds they have you sign this touch pad to say you have received your medications. Under the spot where I signed it read, "Do you need counseling? Yes or No?" I said, "I don't know. I'm picking up anxiety meds so maybe I do need counseling."

From the time my daughter was four, our family has been guided in our spectrum education from outside the home by dedicated men and women of early childhood intervention programs created to help families like ours learn to adapt, cope, and grow together as a family. More than once I've shot prayers of gratitude heavenward for their support. Believe me, when you are beginning the process of identifying your children's difficulties and struggles, it is easy to feel overwhelmed and uncertain of what is best for your family. It meant the world to me that these specialists existed in my community and helped my children get to where they needed to be so that they might receive services quickly. I would be much more of a mess if it weren't for their kind intervention.

I only discovered there were programs available for developmentally delayed children thanks to a friend from church. She had substitute taught Rebekah's youth class one Sunday when another teacher was ill. After careful observation, she noted several behaviors the other children the same age as my daughter exhibited in class, that Rebekah had not. She recommended that I contact a local organization, Kids on the Move (KOTM), that empowers families through early intervention and early head start programs for developmentally delayed children. I trust my friend, and I know that she loves my family dearly, so I contacted the organization.

Within a few weeks, a worker from Kids on the Move came into my home to explain the testing process. They would send over occupational therapists, speech therapists, psychologists, and more to interview our children and us to identify possible areas of concern. Based on those test results, we would then establish an in-home program with goals for the family to work towards. Then the individual professionals would come in and teach all of us how to play and interact with one another in a way that would strengthen our bond and increase our children's learning curve in a way that met their needs. As the program was subsidized by the government, the program would either be free or relatively inexpensive based on our income and number of family members in the home.

There was only one problem—Rebekah was too old for the program. The organization focused on helping families with kids from birth until they turned three years of age. After their third birthday, the children would transition to the local school district's early learning programs. Even though she didn't qualify for their program, Kids on the Move did help me get Rebekah transitioned quickly into the integrated preschool near our home by walking me through the process step by step and setting up all necessary appointments. However, because they had come into our home to observe and assess our family, several of the specialists noticed early warning autism signs in Colin and recommended getting him enrolled in their program.

These trained professionals taught us about sensory signals, obstructive play, food therapy, and so much more, in our own home, several times a month. The program even provided counseling services for me to help cope with the sudden onslaught of emotions that comes from finding out your children aren't "normal." I cannot emphasize enough how these men and women saved my mommy bacon. I learned how to wrap Colin tightly in a blanket when he is stressed out, so that his body feels protected to where it could calm down. They taught me how to sit down on the floor with him and observe, looking for hand gestures and body language that signaled he wanted me in his play world. We discovered the physical activities that worked best for my son personally (swinging, jumping, etc.) to help him then focus on what we wanted him to learn. We were taught in our own safe environment in a way that met the needs of our specific family. But beyond that I learned how miraculous it can be for my son to look at me with his clear water blue eyes—actually look at me for the first time since he was born. It was only then, that he said, "I love you." Those three words were rare, but I learned to cherish them in those moments that mother and child connected so deeply Colin's mind would clear enough to say them. Thanks to Kids on the Move, I learned to look for those cherished moments and honor them.

Now here's a confession for you—when Colin transitioned into the preschool program I was sad to lose the in-home support system and teaching that I so desperately needed. KOTM got me. They understood our family. And they helped us to excel. I went into a sort of withdrawal phase for a few months. Then I had one of those brainstorm moments of desperation that led me to call on KOTM once more to test my Joseph. So far, I was zero for two. I had no typical kids to compare my youngest to. Sure, Joseph was behaving in similar ways as Rebekah and Colin, but I honestly couldn't tell if he was mimicking their behavior, or if he was truly delayed as well. When the testing process resulted in Joseph being severely developmentally delayed, I jumped for joy, trying to hide my relief that I wasn't just being a goober.

I was truly zero for three; all my kids had special needs. It wasn't just me. And strange person that I am, I was happy.

Chapter Fourteen

Musical Mayhem

Colin was playing on his Kindle the other night and was so giddy. I'm not sure what app it was, but it was playing Beatles songs. He was leaping and bouncing around the hallway and would come running up to the gate singing at the top of his lungs, 'All you need is love.' I couldn't help but laugh and cry at the same time. Huge thanks to the Beatles for helping my son shine.

One thing I've learned about my kids over the years is that they learn best when taught in multi-sensory engaging activities. Since our children started showing signs of developmental delays when they were toddlers, we learned to watch *a lot* of educational television—*Baby Signing Time, Blue's Clue's, Jack's Big Music Show,* and *Your Baby Can Read* to name a few. Most of these shows teach children through auditory (music), visual (labeling objects), kinesthetic (movement/activity/dance), etc. I would sit on the floor or the couch as my kids hopped like bunnies all around me, laughing and soaking up every ounce of learning they could from these shows.

When we weren't watching educational television, we were singing the songs in the car, or working on activities that reinforced what we would learn. My husband and I even used the sign language we were learning with the children to help Colin to communicate what he wanted to us.

My husband and I were happy our children were gaining skills through music education as we've always been musically inclined as a couple. In college, Frank earned duel bachelor's degrees in computers and music. He loved music so much that if a band director had an instrument, but no one available to play it, Frank taught himself. That is how he learned flute, percussion, sousaphone, trombone, and several other instruments.

Figure 24 - Rebekah and Colin playing piano - 2010

Whereas, I have always been into singing. Growing up I'd drive my parents nuts reciting all the songs from commercials for Oscar Mayer (though I am not a fan of hot dogs), McDonald's, and more. Since grade school, I have participated in several choirs, and for a short while took piano and voice lessons, often earning decent recognition and awards for my singing.

My piano skills were frustrating for my parents and teacher alike. I would attend lessons only to return home, practice half-heartedly once, and then put the music away. Then, just prior to my next lesson, I would retrieve the hidden music which (according to my mother) I played perfectly, thus driving her batty. I have never been able to play to the written speed of the music, nor stay within a consistent beat,

Figure 25 - Colin learning how to use sousaphone valves - 2010

instead I've always played the music how I *felt* the rhythm should flow. I keep what musical skills I have focused on choral singing and making up random songs about pretty much everything from brushing teeth to waking up in the morning and waiting for the school bus. My kids so love it—not!

Frank and I were thrilled that the kids excelled in their education with learning through videos incorporating music. It became natural for Frank to follow up an episode of *Jack's Big Music Show* in which the Little Bad Wolf learned to play the tuba by bringing out his sousaphone for the babies how to play.

The rules of music were consistent. Music has rules. Music made sense; it was a very cause-and-affect activity—if you press this button, this will change the sound; if you blow in the mouthpiece, you will make a sound (maybe not always the best sound, but a sound nonetheless). Music they could understand.

People? Well, that's another story.

Figure 26 - Rebekah investigating daddy's sousaphone - 2010

Chapter Fifteen

Science at Home

Things you never thought you'd say to your kids: "Go find me the dog's liver please."

My kids are weird, and I love them for it. They love Easter for the egg hunts and Halloween for the trick or treating. They love the act of finding and receiving candy, but that doesn't mean they will eat it. And I'm okay with that, except for one problem—it leaves the bulk of the candy for Frank and me to eat (not the best outcome for my hips).

On the other hand, my kids are scientists at heart. They understand logic (well, their form of logic). They comprehend that investigating an object or a concept requires testing hypotheses to confirm the expected results. If a different outcome is produced, then you create a new theory and work through the process again. So when my friend, Loralee Leavitt, was working on her book *Candy Experiments 2*, she asked my daughter and I if we could verify her results by experimenting on candy in our own home. We would get rid of the candy, learn cool science while doing it, and I didn't have to eat the leftovers—count me in.

Rebekah and I browsed through the list of experiments, picking a new one every single day. We dissolved gummy worms and turned them into Jell-O. We baked marshmallow peeps to see them expand. And we learned all about chemical changes and what causes them. Oh, my goodness, we had so much fun being the mother/daughter science team testing out truths in our very own kitchen. We were like science superheroes—at least in my daughter's own eyes, and that is good enough for me.

When we were done, we sent the results off to Loralee. You should have seen the sparkle in Rebekah's eyes the day I brought home the completed copy of my friend's book after it was released. I truly was a superhero that day. Since then, whenever I go into my daughter's room I see the book lying next to her pillow in the big stack of science books, foreign language dictionaries, and joke books that she keeps on hand. Even years later, when Easter and Halloween roll around, we eagerly whip out copies of *Candy Experiments 1* and *Candy Experiments 2* and plot what masterful experiments we will perform on our next haul of candy.

******

How do we explain the concept of riding bikes without training wheels in our house? SCIENCE.

My kids figure things out mentally before they can be open to the physical experience. We are teaching the science of balance, gravity, friction, inertia, etc. so that in a month or two Rebekah might be comfortable with taking the training wheels off her bike.

We then back our science instruction up with some very fun family time watching *Bill Nye the Science Guy* on Netflix. My kids are fully enamored.

Yep, science is how we roll in the Pellett household. Wait, then why did God send my kids a writer for a mother? Maybe it is so their mother will finally learn scientific concepts.

******

Once upon a time, eons ago (aka back in my beginning years of college), I was studying to be a marine biologist. I wanted desperately to work out on the ocean, studying whales and dolphins. There were a handful of problems with this dream: 1) I lived in the desert, and 2) I flunked microbiology. Then one day while I was in my bedroom studying for midterms, I heard my roommate come home carrying several grocery bags.

I went back to my studying until I heard a squeal and my roommate, who was from Beijing but was studying abroad in the United States, came running into my room. "I need your help," she said. "I have a problem."

I followed Cindy back into the kitchen where I found a fish in my sink, very much alive.

"I need you to kill it," she said.

"Say what?" I asked, taking several steps away from the flopping fish.

"You're studying to be a biologist. I need you to kill it."

It turns out she had gone to the Asian market and ordered what she thought was frozen fish to make fish soup with, but when she got it home, she realized that it was still alive. Since I was going to be a biologist, I should be able to kill it for her, right?

Nope. I switched majors the very next day. In the end, I moved out to New England to be closer to the ocean, but where I graduated with a degree in professional writing instead of marine biology, and I was okay with that.

So, when my kids were born with a natural love for science, I was in trouble. Until my mother-in-law moved in. When my father-in-law passed away, my mother-in-law stayed with us for a few months to give her time to regain her footing. The beautiful side effect of that move is that she is a scientist—a geologist—and my kids *love* science.

Grandma would whip out scientific principles on a regular basis and pass on her knowledge to my children. The children loved the hands-on learning as she showed them her collections of animal skulls and skeleton replicas. And for her birthday, we even surprised her by getting her a display of Indonesian insects that I wouldn't normally let anywhere near my house—I mean the spider was gargantuan. Yuck. But with the amazing collection came certain difficulties with my children. Colin loves to explore, touch, and take a part objects to better understand them. He would sneak into Grandma's closet where she kept the best science stuff hidden and open the bags, leaving animal body parts spread all over the upstairs. I swear I spent most of July looking for animal intestines and livers.

But one of the best memories is when we performed the diet cola/Mentos experiment with the kids. My mother-in-law had purchased a cylinder with a spring-loaded release for dropping the mint candy into a two-liter bottle of diet cola. The kids were bouncing-of-the-walls excited; they'd seen this experiment before on *Mythbusters* and couldn't wait to test it out for themselves.

The difficulty was figuring out how to implement the experiment in a townhome with three kids on the spectrum. Our backyard was not

big enough for the pending geysers, but if we took our kids out front, they would lose focus while we setup and run off—Rebekah to find her friends, Colin to check out one of the neighbors' houses, and Joseph into the street. The adults concocted a plan. Grandma bought the supplies, Frank set up the experiment out in the communal grassy area while the kids and I watched from the opened living room window. Then, once Frank had

Figure 27 - Science experiment with Joseph - 2016

prepared the first bottle, he called out the children one at a time.

First up was Rebekah. Joseph and Colin stood on the window seal, their faces pressed against the window screen until their noses were smooshed flat, to ensure the best view of the experiment. Frank slid the Mentos-filled cylinder into the mouth of the cola bottle and stepped away. Rebekah pressed the latch, releasing the candy into the soda and jumped back to a safe distance. A tower of brown, foaming liquid soared into the sky accompanied by squeals of delight from Rebekah.

"That is *so* cool," she screamed, giving daddy a hug before running back into the house.

As Frank set up the second bottle, I unlocked the door for Rebekah and ushered Joseph out for his turn. As his experiment exploded into the air, he jumped up and down, his cheeks flushed with joy and yelled, "I wanna do it again."

"Nope, the last bottle is for Colin," Frank said.

Unlocking the door once again, I moved aside just in time for Colin to rush outside, and for me to drag Joseph in. Colin slowly circled the grass, eyeing the two emptied bottles and inspecting the one meant for him. He began to giggle as Frank placed the Mentos into their cylinder. When the cylinder was placed into the nozzle of the soda, Colin backed up five feet and covered his ears with his hands.

Figure 28 - Rebekah and Joseph watching Colin perform the diet cola / Mentos experiment - Summer 2016

"Do you want to push the button?" Frank asked him, motioning to the activation latch that would start the experiment.

Colin mumbled, "No" but stepped toward the bottle as if eager to try. Finally, after a minute of coaxing, Colin leaped in, pushing the release button before jumping back to relative safety. As the diet cola soared into the air Colin erupted in a series of giggles and acrobatics that would have been at home in Cirque du Soleil.

That's my boy, I thought, feeling choked up inside.

Never would I have thought that science, my failed college dream, would help me connect more fully with my special needs children. I may still not understand all the rules and complexity surrounding it, but I will always have a cherished place in my heart for science helping me to connect with my children.

Figure 29 - The results of Colin's experiment.

Chapter Sixteen

Save My Soul

My counselor told me I don't so much need help with knowing how to deal with being a mom of special needs kids, but coming to the realization that I'm actually a pretty awesome mom. I broke down crying when she said that.

I love church. I love the uplifting nature of church. I love having the reminders of what is truly important in life, and I love the feeling of peace I get when I go to church. But ever since I had children (even before I learned they were all special needs), I struggled with how to keep my children reverent during sacrament meeting. I always felt like the biggest failure because my kids were the ones screaming, jumping, and talking loudly. It was especially hard when we had little Joseph. The kids out numbered the adults. We did not have enough hands. Then, shortly after Colin was born, Frank was called to be the music leader in the main worship service. Suddenly, I feared going to church and having to deal with the children all by myself.

It got to the point that it was almost a relief if my kids got sick because then I could stay home to take care of them without dreading that they would disrupt the services and make it harder for everyone else to feel the spirit and peace I so longed for at church. But the more often that my kids got sick, the more I missed the peaceful spirit I felt from attending worship service, and being able to partake of the sacrament.

But on the few occasions we successfully made it to worship church, I was left to sit alone with two kids two and under for the entire first hour while my husband sat up in the seats behind the pulpit. While he seemed to be peacefully enjoying the meeting, I would usually end up bruised, battered, and in tears.

Sitting alone with my children felt like being the referee in the middle of a WWF wrestling match. While I grappled with Rebekah in one hand, trying to keep her from whacking her head on the pew in front of us, my other hand was restraining Colin so that he could not escape underneath everyone's feet and out the back door. While Frank listened intently to the members of the congregation who took turns teaching us, I could barely hear a single word as I struggled to keep either children from starting an all-out offensive on each other.

Please do not get me wrong—my husband was an excellent chorister; being music director was the perfect calling for him. He not only led the congregational hymns, but also directed the church choir, giving him a fantastic opportunity to extend and build his skills in music. I'm very grateful that he had that chance. But he had that calling for *three* years. That meant I endured my bright, rambunctious, tenacious toddlers during my entire pregnancy with Joseph—through morning sickness, migraines, fatigue, and, well, you get the point.

I also meant dealing with my kids' social anxieties. Since my kids see the world differently and behave accordingly, they struggle through situations that require them to be social, follow body language, or unclear expectations. They thrive on consistency, routine, and clear expectations. People tend to be the opposite on the whole. So being thrust into such a public situation with a large congregation was daunting, confusing, and a bit nerve wracking for all of us.

To help compensate for the stress Rebekah felt in attending church, she often brought her bunny, a stuffed animal my mother had given me for my children prior to my first miscarriage. When Rebekah was born, she inherited the bunny, which quickly became her perfect anxiety solution. When asked what her stuffed animal's name is, Rebekah would look up at the individual with her petite brows furrowed, and a confused look in her eyes. "Bunny," she would reply sincerely. Rebekah simply was not able to understand why an animal (stuffed or otherwise) would be named anything other than what it was. The bigger Rebekah grew, the more tattered, gray, and well-loved her bunny became. And if she ever forgot bunny at home, she was unable to soothe herself enough to endure three hours of worship service.

There were many times we went home early. And if any of the children were ever sick, then I would stay home with them so that Frank could go lead music. In all honesty, the only reason we survived the times we did make it to church were because of my friend Sonya and her three lovely daughters—Nalissa, Camryn and Hannah. Sonya's teenage daughters were my regular go to babysitters; they knew my kids, they understood my kids, and my kids are always excited every single time they come over to babysit. Every week Sonya and her family would save us a seat in the pew directly behind them. If we didn't arrive by five minutes until services started, then they'd give up our seat to anyone who needed it.

But if we did arrive, then they became my instant lifesavers. Anytime someone had a meltdown, even if it was me, Sonya or her girls would come back and sit with the other kids, while I took the necessary culprit out to the foyer for a breather. If a baby needed distracting so that I could help a toddler practice better reverence, then Sonya would lift the baby over the pew, so that I would have my hands free to help the older ones.

The day my husband was released from his calling, I cried. I was so relieved and happy. I felt like my Superman had returned to me, lifting a dump-truck from off my shoulders. I fully believe that the only reason I survived the three years without him was due to Sonya and her family. If there were ever an example of angels on earth, I found it in Sonya and her daughters. Without their service, my spiritual cup would have drained long ago, instead of overflowing with blessings. But because of their service I also learned the value of swallowing my pride so that I might be served by those in a position to help. I only hope one day I may be able to pay it forward to another family who needs an understanding heart to help them survive church.

Goofy Break —Part 4

Because We Can

Hidden Gems

There is nothing quite like walking along with one of my children and they're simply holding my hand. That rare precious moment when they aren't trying to pull me on ahead or trying to escape. That simple few sacred seconds when we're just walking, and I look down at them, and they look up at me and grin. Those moments are priceless. I was blessed with one this morning.

The randomness of life can illuminate a hidden gem in a family's overall personality. To truly see how brilliantly wonderful our family is, take a peak at these random silly moments.

******

An often phrase used lately in our house "Stop trying to smother your brother." That's what you get when two little boys do a ton of wrestling.

******

Out of context quote of the day: "Get that fork out of your bum."

******

This morning I went to wake up Rebekah and read scriptures with her.

My little Joseph comes into the room and says, "Mommy, are you ready to play ouch?"

I said, "Sure. How do you play?"

Joseph holds up his right knee by both hands and starts hoping around the bedroom saying, "Ouch! Ouch! Ouch!"

My little comedian. Too true, but way too funny. I nearly fell of the bed.

******

My daughter and I were in the living room watching a movie. She was lying on the couch watching, while I was sitting in the recliner. She rolled over and her blanket fell on the floor.

Rebekah: Mom, can you pick up the blanket I dropped and put it back on me?

Me: No.

Rebekah: But you can do it because you're the greatest mom.

Me: Part of being the greatest mom is teaching my daughter when she is perfectly capable to do something herself.

Rebekah: Are you talking about me?

Me: Yes, I am.

Rebekah: Ugh.

*****

At bedtime, we leave our door open, but put up a child gate to signal that it is time to wind down for the night (aka mommy is off the clock). Colin came up to the security gate on our bedroom door one night and said, "Firewood please."

I looked over the brim of my book and replied, "Um . . .no. It's bedtime, and we don't have a fireplace."

******

"Mom, I want the marble run," Joseph said, pointing to a picture in a catalog.

The toy was well out of our price range and we were nowhere near his birthday. I shook my head, and handed the catalog back to him. "I'm sorry, honey, but no."

"Why not?"

Too tired to translate, I explained, "Because our expenses outweigh our income."

"Oh, you mean we're broke?" he asked.

"That's right, sweetie. But you sure are a smart kid to be able to translate what I said to a meaning you understood."

"Why thank you, Mom."

"You're welcome, Joseph."

But did this stop the same child from asking for the same marble run thirty minutes later? Not a chance.

******

After a week of being confined upstairs due to illness, I think Rebekah might be feeling a bit better. She just yelled down from her bedroom, "You know Mom, you can't keep me up here forever."

******

When I picked up Frank and the kids from band practice, I told him the kitchen and our bathroom smelled like vomit and I couldn't figure out why.

Rebekah asked, "What is vomit?"

We explained to her what it meant using synonyms.

Then when she was getting ready for bed she said, "But I don't want to go to the bathroom if it smells like Vermont."

I laughed, then replied, "Vomit honey, not Vermont. And it was MY bathroom, not yours. Yours is safe to use."

"Oh, okay," she replied.

Then Frank said, "Poor Vermont."

******

Yesterday Rebekah was playing with my arms and waddling my excess skin and said, "I wanna be older so that I can have flabby arms."

Today Rebekah showed me that if I paid close attention that her belly jiggled and you could hear her drink sloshing around inside. Then she said, "Mom, just like your arms."

******

Frank put on *Mythbusters* to watch as a family and Joseph said, "Way to go, you AMAZING Daddy!"

Now that's parenting done right.

******

Last year, when I would drop Rebekah off at school, I would tell her, "I love you more than the Universe."

Lately, I've been telling her, "I love you more than salad. And I love you more than chocolate." She would always reply in a teenager-type tone, "MOM!" But she knows how much I love a good salad and how I'm addicted to chocolate.

Tonight, I added, "I love you more than pizza." She asked me why I loved her more than pizza. I told her it's because she was remarkable and that I was glad she was my daughter. She replied, "Aww! That is so sweet." And then she fell asleep.

I may not always be sure my feelings are communicated well to my children who understand language very differently than I do, but sometimes I think we actually connect (even if it is through unusual means). Tonight is one of those times.

******

I was sitting next to Rebekah pretending to be asleep and snoring when she grabbed my hand and blew a raspberry on it. I asked her, "What did you do that for?" She replied, "For free."

******

I just got a steam burn on my arm from making the kids mac 'n cheese for lunch. While I cooled it under water, Frank came in to finish getting lunch ready. He told Rebekah about me burning my arm and suggested she ask if I was okay or to possibly kiss my arm.

Rebekah replied, "I can't do that, my lips will get hot."

******

I was on the phone with my mom in my bedroom when Rebekah came in and said, "Mom, I spilled. I need a towel."

I replied, "There's one in my bathroom hanging on the wall."

Rebekah said, "I can't go in there. There are ghosts."

Me: "So turn on the light. That will make the ghosts go away."

Rebekah goes to my bathroom door and turns on the light and yells, "Go away ghosts!" and then promptly gets the towel hanging on the rack. Running back out she quickly flips the lights off and just before she slams the door shut she yells, "GOODNIGHT GHOSTS!!!"

******

I got the kids a tangram puzzle (a puzzle involving the manipulation of geometric shapes to form images of houses, flowers, birds, etc.) to work on. Unfortunately, I was getting the names of the shapes all wrong, and it has led to a series of bad puns between Frank and I.

1) I said, "I'm sorry Rebekah. I was looking at the blue shape at the wrong angle." Rebekah asked, "What does the angle say?" And Frank replied, "I don't know, but I bet it was acute."

2) Rebekah asked which shape she should do next, and I suggested the rhombus. When she asked why the rhombus, I replied, "Because I don't know how to tango."

******

Usually when Rebekah is frustrated we tell her "Stop! Breathe! And don't freak out then ask mom and dad to help you out."

But just now I heard her say while she was doing imagine play "Stop! Breathe! And Dance!"

I like her version better.

Section Five:

To Err Is Human,

To Do Laundry Divine

Chapter Seventeen

Mattress Slides

Some days you pick your battles. Other days you get out your camera.

What is a mattress for? For sliding of course.

When our children were little, our pediatrician told us that kids in general should average between twelve to fourteen hours of sleep between naps and bedtime combined. But, no matter when we put the kids to bed, Colin is usually the last to fall asleep and the first to wake in the morning. We tried earlier bed times and later bedtimes to no avail. We even tried liquid melatonin on the doctor's recommendation to help him fall asleep easier; Colin loves the flavor, but continues to laugh in the face of sleep even after taking it for two years.

Nothing worked. Only then did our doctor tell us that autistic children tend to need less sleep. Instead, Colin spends his time finding creative uses for everyday items like his bed by turning it into a trampoline, or better yet, a slide.

Then, one night, we were downstairs when we heard the boys laughing. I turned to Frank and said, "I guess I should be glad they're playing together." But out of curiosity I went upstairs to see what mischief they were creating. As I crested the last set of stairs to the landing I discovered that the linen closet had been stripped clean, until all its contents were strewn across the floor and Colin's mattress lay on top like a cherry on top of an ice-cream sundae. And where my sheets had once been neatly folded and stored in the linen closet, my two little boys were happily resting on the emptied shelves. I forced myself to breathe, so that I wouldn't yell.

That was the beginning of a new routine in our household: every few days my little monkeys would get into a mischievous mood and create a mattress slide. But unlike the version in *The Princess Diaries 2: Royal Engagement* where Princess Mia and her friends sit on the mattresses as they slide down the castle stairs, my boys created a mountain out of the mattress. The creative process goes as follows:

1) Break into the linen closet in the upstairs hallway (removing the safety latch or the entire closet door from its hinges if needed).

2) Empty the shelves of all contents until they are naked.

3) Get Joseph to help construct a trail of blankets, towels, sheets, and tablecloths leading from the closet and into shared bedroom.

4) Expertly yank Colin's mattress off of the lower bunk, laying it carefully on top of linen trail.

5) Position body on top and roll down mattress, out the door, and into the linen closet.

6) When a break is needed, climb up the empty shelves like a ladder and rest until recovered.

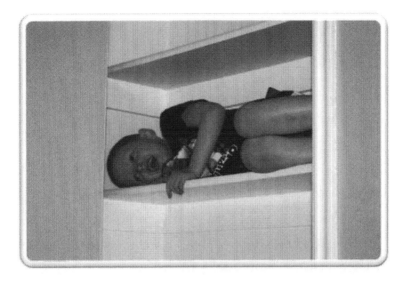

Figure 30 - Colin resting while mattress sliding - 2015

7) Repeat for hours.

8) When mommy discovers the mess, ham it up for effect so she will retrieve her camera instead of doling out well-deserved restrictions.

Figure 31 - Joseph upping the cute factor to get out of trouble

With his next attempt at a mattress slide a week later, Colin had taken everything out of the linen closet upstairs and dumped it in a pile on the floor. I put it all back, then went to lie down for a bit. When I returned, he'd done it again. This time Colin had dumped everything in his room between his bed and the door frame. I was beyond frustrated.

Colin took one look at me and said, "Uh oh."

I zipped my mouth shut, walked into my room and locked the door. I just couldn't handle it right then. A little while later, Rebekah came and knocked on my door and said we had visitors. When I came out I could see that Colin had added to his creation by dumping all the stuffed animals in the house on top, followed by his mattress. At the end of the ramp he'd laid the safety gate. Colin had formed a slide/ramp from his bunkbed down into the hallway so that he could roll into the now emptied linen closet out in the upstairs foyer. Once his masterpiece was finished, Colin would climb up to Joseph's upper bunk and jump to the mountain below, then roll down the length of his boy-made hill. Part of me was quite impressed by his ingenuity, part of me was exasperated, and part of me wanted to scream.

Figure 32 – The boys' bedroom post mattress slide incident

Even years later, Colin continues to find great joy from pulling the linens out of the closet. Sometimes he will make his slide, and other times he builds a soft mountain to kick back and relax on as he plays his Kindle. I still struggle every single time he does it. My mind instantly swerves to *Look at all that hard work that will have to be redone.* While I'm sure my son's mind is thinking, *I have created something glorious.*

I've come to the conclusion that Colin really *needs* the sensory only a mountain of clean laundry can provide him. And, if I looked at it from his perspective, the mountain of towels and blankets did look pretty cozy. But I desired a safe passage through my hallway. So I tried for a compromise: I removed all the table cloths and blankets that have special meaning for me and hid them elsewhere in the house. Then, I gave myself permission to *not* get frustrated when he took out anything that remained.

Within a day of implementing the compromise Colin found where we'd stashed the other blankets and pulled them out, and stuffed them back into the floor of the linen closet to sit on.

For my second compromise, I cleaned out the closet in the boys' bedroom and piled all the blankets into a mountain inside. (My children looked at me as if I'd gone insane.) Feeling proud of myself I went to bed.

The next morning, I found Joseph fast asleep on the floor of the empty linen closet. So I've decided that it just might be time to purge our lesser used items into plastic bins and store them away from inquisitive eyes. I'm not about to delude myself that this is the perfect solution, it is far from. But do I really want to destroy my health and my relationship with my children over a pile of laundry? I choose not to.

Chapter Eighteen

To Dye Is Human

You can predict what type of day it will turn out to be when Ben & Jerry's is a viable option for breakfast.

Each person copes with stress in their own way; I am a professional stress eater and stress shopper. Trust me, when trying to raise money for equipment to deal with my children's sensory needs I can inhale an entire bag of Oreos before you can say gourmet cupcake bake sale.

Stress. Eat. Repeat. That's me.

Another quick, easy coping mechanism that I frequent is dyeing my hair. Give me a four dollar box of Clairol, and watch out world. This chick's hair can go mahogany red in less time than it takes to get my kids to go to sleep. Side note: I must remember to never go blond again or try to repair a bad home dye job myself. Orange is not flattering on this face.

When I was about to turn forty, I was so stressed I designed my own mid-life crisis. I signed up for my first ever 5K run (more like turtle crawl) and begged my hair stylist neighbor to dye my hair a glorious variation of magenta to deep purple. When I walked in the door my kids took one look and said, "Pretty. Now change it back."

Let the punishment and smack talk begin. Even though I had given them fair notice of the pending change, it was more than their little minds could cope. Have I mentioned yet that my kids don't like change? If I haven't, then guess what? My kids DON'T LIKE CHANGE! And when life feels out of control, they get out of control.

Imagine a family of monkeys who've had their bananas taken away and a mango just won't cut it. Now multiply that by infinity.

I almost caved under the pressure: the leap in personal expression through hair color was more daring for me than I care to admit. But when a laundry accident sent Clorox bleach flying all over my hair, face, clothes, and even into my mouth a few days post-dye job, I begged my neighbor to spend another four hours repairing the damage.

When the morning of the race arrived, my running partner picked me up and ran me through racing protocol. Even though I had sprained my leg just a month before, I didn't care. I felt spunky, enlivened, and free to face the world. Who cares that my hair and face were the same sparkly tones as I hobbled through the race. I still wear that finishers medal with pride (just hidden under my Spanx thank you very much). I wanted to prove to my kids that you can accomplish scary hard things, even if you stalling halfway up that middle-aged hill.

My daring husband piled two toddlers in a stroller with the third on top to greet me as I stumbled across the finish line. Their cheers meant more to me than I can ever express. Almost as much as my daughter bragging about me at church the next day (though I could barely move without a thousand muscles screaming damnation in retaliation to my success). And I still proudly admire that one remarkable photo the race photographer snagged as I neared the home stretch, breaking into a run just in time to be captured in the perfect race photo, though I had walked the previous 90 percent of the course.

In the end, I'd do it all again. Just to see that sparkle in my daughter's eyes when she realized that if mommy could do hard things at forty, then she could do hard things too.

Chapter Nineteen

The Tooth Fairy Dilemma

"I feel so accomplished today, I put in my contacts, and that is something I haven't done since Mother's Day."
—*Karen Pellett*

The tooth fairy must have some serious questions about our family.

My kids love a good tussle—I don't know if it gives them the extra sensory input they require or what, but they often get into brawls that would make an MMA fighter proud. Just yesterday we enjoying outside time, waiting for the various rides to schools. Bouncing on the balls of his tennis shoes, Joseph yelled, "I gotta go potty." So, I asked my daughter to keep an eye on Colin to make sure he didn't go into the street while I rushed Joseph inside to do his duty before his bus arrived. Emergency averted, I was helping Joseph get on his backpack as we were walking back outside. And what to my wandering eyes should appear, but my older son in a choke hold as his sister wrestles him onto the grass.

"Do NOT strangle your brother!" I yelled, kicking into running mode. Once I made sure that Colin was indeed still breathing, I turned to Rebekah and asked her what had happened. She looked up at me with big, brown eyes that would melt your heart and replied, "I was keeping him out of the street like you asked."

Now roll back the calendar by four years: my daughter was five, my son three. Rebekah comes running into the living room, tears streaking down her cherubic face, and crying like an injured banshee. Pulling her into a hug, I asked her what happened.

Burying her curly mop of hair into my shoulder, she sobbed. "COLIN PUNCHED ME!"

"Where did he punch you, hon," I asked.

"Upstairs."

"Oh, sweetie," I said, trying not to laugh at her literalness. I tilted her chin up, so I could see her face. "Where does it hurt?"

Rebekah opened her mouth and started wiggling her bottom front teeth. "He punched me here, and now my teeth are going to fall out."

I remember when I was a kid and bad things would happen, even if by accident, it was the end of the world (at least for that moment). I remember how valid my emotions were. But as a tired mom, I struggle to remember at times what true childhood tragedy feels like and how reason is nonexistent. A child will believe what they believe and often will not change their opinion until someone (other than their parents) explain things to them. So, when my daughter's teeth became loose as a direct result of her brother's actions, she was going to be toothless for the rest of her life and beyond.

Nothing I said calmed her internal raging storm. Until I talked to my neighbor. My neighbors are brilliant, astounding, and understanding people. This particular neighbor had a son just a year or two older than my daughter, who could've been Superman in my daughter's eyes (don't tell them I told you so). When I told this particular friend about Rebekah being devastated that her teeth were loose because her little brother had punched her, my friend offered to bring her son over for a visit.

With two raps on our door, my salvation arrived. In walked Noah, one of the kindest and smartest boys I know. I brought over my suddenly shy daughter to say hi. I explained what had happened, and Noah grinned and showed off his missing teeth to my daughter. Opening wide, he said, "If you look close, you see this thing poking through my gums? That's the new tooth. So, don't worry. If your teeth fall out, your big teeth will come in."

I watched as my daughter's shoulders relaxed and the tension left her body. If Noah said it will be fine, then everything was going to be good.

With their sensory needs, my kids investigate everything from asphalt to hair ties to Barbies by putting them in their mouth, years after teething rings lost their interest. So it was no surprise to me when, three months later, my daughter was sitting in the living room watching television and chomping down on a chip clip. Rebekah had been chewing on an alligator style chip clip while immersed in watching the *Wild Kratts* DVD we'd checked out from the local library when she jumped back with a start, then spit out her two front teeth. Those loose baby teeth offenders had wiggled their last.

As I washed off the clip, I told her about the time-honored tooth fairy tradition. Her eyes lit up like they do when she is truly happy. We ran and got an envelope and placed her teeth carefully inside. Sealing it up, we set it on top of the piano bench, which was sitting on top of the piano so that her brothers wouldn't find them.

"Remind me tonight, and we'll put it under your pillow," I told her. "Then in the morning we'll see what the tooth fairy left you as a prize."

Um, three weeks later I found the envelope still sitting on top of the piano bench. We'd both forgotten. I found Rebekah up in her room and we both face palmed ourselves before promptly placing the envelope under her pillow.

I gave her a hug then ran downstairs quickly. Leaning over the armrest of the couch I whispered to Frank, "I need to run to the store for an emergency pack of Tooth Fairy Pokémon cards." To the kids, I yelled, "I'm off to Wal-Mart."

As I opened the back door, Rebekah called down, "Don't forget to buy you and me some patience pills while you're there."

If only they sold them there. When I got home I told my daughter, "I looked and looked, and it seems Wal-Mart just doesn't carry patience pills. I guess we'll have to do it the old-fashioned way and practice it."

But at least they had the Pokémon cards. Later that night, I crept into my daughter's room and traded the much-desired Pokémon playing cards for the wayward teeth. *Man, the tooth-fairy has changed her rules since my day*, I thought. With a kiss on Rebekah's forehead, I turned and slipped out into the night unnoticed. *My work here is done.*

******

When it comes to losing teeth, Colin is a pro. He is so skilled that he doesn't even tell us that he's lost them in the first place. I don't know how many times I'll be playing with my kids and Colin's face will light up with joy, and I'll tilt my head to the side, and think, *What's different with this picture?* A few minutes later the night light clicks on in my brain. *He's missing another tooth.*

I don't know if he swallows them, tosses them down the drain, or what. Only twice in three years have I discovered a missing tooth abandoned on the floor or in the folds of the Mario Kart blanket on his bed. I don't think it even occurs to Colin that he should tell anyone; it's just something that happens, and then you move on.

As for braving the dentist . . . HA! It took me five years to gather the courage to even think about taking Colin.

The first time I did, Colin was fine in the waiting room, but as soon as we walked back toward the exam room he covered his ears, yelled, "No!" and tried to run out. I veered him into the little room and told him I'd be right there with him, but he refused to get into the chair. Instead, I sat down and held him on my lap. Poor Colin kept his hands over his ears and yelled, "No!" The hygienist went ahead and skipped the pictures and cleaning and went straight to bringing the dentist in.

He was able to get Colin to briefly say, "Ahhh."

"Well, he has a molar coming in," the dentist said, setting his mirror back on the metal tray.

And that was all we could do. The dentist said we'd work Colin up slowly to being comfortable there. In the meantime, I should try to make sure he flosses at least once a week.

A year later, Colin survived having pictures taken of his two front teeth. The dentist admitted defeat and recommended we take my son to a pediatric dentist specialist for sedation dentistry. Several of my friends who have autistic children have had negative experiences coming out of anesthesia, so I was nervous. But since my son's idea of how to use a toothbrush was to brush his teeth for ten seconds then scrub the toilet and clean the walls with his toothbrush before putting it back in his mouth to finish the job, I agreed.

The place we chose was heaven for kids, complete with video games, movies, headphones, comfy seating, and more, all wrapped in a soothing beach-themed office with a surfboard mounted on the waiting room wall. It was playland for our son, but murder on our already empty wallets. Our down payment (yes, like a down payment on a car) was over eight hundred dollars, after insurance and before the anesthetist.

On the day of Colin's appointment, he couldn't eat anything for twelve hours before hand. My brave and valiant husband took the day off of work, and accepted the challenge of keeping Colin from snacking on anything (gravel, chalk, and dirt included). They played at the park, and ran errands to Home Depot. Just before dentist time they picked me up. After signing our lives away on paperwork, Colin, Frank, and I retired to a back room where my son could sit on my lap and watch television. Then, when he was most comfortable, the anesthetist poked Colin in the arm with a needle that had him slumped in my arms like a rag doll in under a minute. Two hours, a full set of x-rays, eight cavities, and two extractions later, the dentist called me back to sit by my son as he sloughed his way out of unconsciousness, so that he awoke to a familiar face.

When Colin opened his eyes, his brows creased, and he frowned. After a few moments, he moved his tongue around his mouth, poking at the gaping spot where his two front teeth had been just that morning. Too tired to care, he slumped into his daddy's arms as Frank carried him out to our car for the short ride home.

I never did see any negative side effects from the sedation. Poor Colin must have been in so much pain prior to getting his teeth fixed because after the surgery he was the happiest he'd been in a long time.

Chapter Twenty

Accident Prone

I wacked my head on the shelf by the stairs while sitting in the racing car ball pit with my two boys. Then Joseph picked up my laptop and said, 'Hey Mom, look!' before throwing it on the ground. Then Colin rode the scooter off the bed in his room and did a face plant into Joseph's bedframe, splitting his lip. Yeah, that's how we roll in the Pellett household.

Insurance companies might seriously want to consider raising rates on health insurance when grown-ups become parents, like they do when teenagers start to drive; the amount of physical damage that occurs from adding children to a home is monumental. Please don't—our pocketbooks are already stretched beyond the breaking point.

But what do you get when you take someone who is an accident waiting to happen and give her three kids on the spectrum? Me. I am so_talented that I can injure myself walking on carpet. Once I even broke my arm on my mother's birthday by running on wet cement during a game of tag where a jacuzzi was home base. Hey, I didn't say I was a smart kid—just a talented one in a very unique field of play.

When I was a kid, I even rode an exercise bicycle all the way to the emergency room from my dining room. Actually, the bolt fell out of the seat, and I flew backwards, landing on my back, crushing the vertebrae in-between my shoulders. Thanks to that incident, I can now dislocate a rib simply by breathing. Told you I was good. In fact, my friend Jessica and I have a running gag about starting a line of clothing made out of bubble wrap to increase the safety of accident-prone people like me.

But nothing prepared me for the damage my body would take when I had kids. I'm not talking about the toll from years of fertility treatments followed by three high risk pregnancies, though that was no picnic. No one told me that an over-sensitized and frustrated three year old would be strong enough to pick up a booster seat and throw it at my head, giving me a concussion. I had no clue that walking my five year old out to the school bus last winter I would slip on ice and screw up my knee so badly that it required surgery to reshape the kneecap.

I've hammered my thumb repairing a battered bookcase worn down by kids trying to climb it. My kids have cracked jokes so funny that I laughed hard enough to hit my noggin on that same bookshelf. I've ruptured a disc in my back putting my baby to bed after a night time feeding, causing localized loss of feeling in my right leg below the knee for five years.

When I tried to lay brickwork to cover a rocky bare patch in our backyard to reduce the number of rocks my son tried to eat, I ended up in the emergency room for dehydration and heatstroke.

And those are just a handful of the dangers of being a spectrum mom. I won't even go into the ones I earned saving my kids from dangerous situations because danger is not a word they understand. Well, maybe I'll tell you just one.

Even making dinner, I'm a hazard to myself. Once I took a sheet pan out of the oven and sit on the counter to cool. Joseph stuck out his tiny hand to touch it, but I stopped him just in time. "It's too hot, honey." When I turned away, he reached for it again. So I grabbed a hot pad and moved the pan up onto a chair on top of the counter. In the act of moving the pan I burned myself creating a six-inch mark on my right forearm in the shape of the Nike symbol.

I wonder if I could get a stipend for being a walking advert for them.

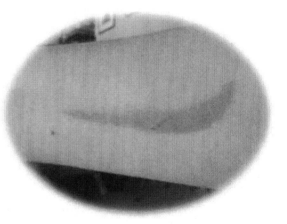

Figure 33 - Burn mark trying to save Joseph from a hot cookie sheet

Summation

Chapter Twenty-One

Observers Wanted

Today while taking pictures of my daughter I leaned in and whispered, 'Right now, to me, you are perfect.' Rebekah reached up, hugged me, placed a tender kiss on my cheek and said, "Aw mom, that is so sweet, but no one is perfect."

Being a parent is not for the faint of heart. Being a parent of special needs kids requires combat training. To be a spectrum parent, you need nerves of steel, faith in people, the power to see and to act upon what you see, and a loving heart.

For those who love someone raising children on the spectrum, the best gift you can ever give those parents is to enter their home graciously, sit down on the floor, be silent, and observe. Watch and wait as the children play. See how they learn, find out how they interact, and be amazed when they let you into their world.

Only after you have spent time in their world, then you should rise, go up to their parents and ask, "Can I give you a hug?" followed by the words, "What do you need me to do?" or "How can I help?"

I promise, you will see our shoulders relax, tears come to our eyes, and our arms (and hearts) open wide was we gladly welcome you into our little piece of the universe.

For careful observers are always wanted and needed.

Figure 34 - Rebekah and Colin watching mommy shoveling snow - Dec 2010

Acknowledgements

I'd like to thank my critique partners and beta readers—Karyn, Rebecca, Adrienne, Ruth, Roxy, Kim, Erika, Jessica, T.J., Betsy, Monique, Ramon, Jenny, Christine, and Angela—for their invaluable feedback on this book. I'm astounded by my cover designer—Ruth Craddock of Green Cloak Design—who, despite being in her third trimester and moving across the country, pulled off an amazing cover and advertisement program.

And, I'm grateful for the team at Eschler Editing for helping *Life as a Spectrum Mom* to shine, and for Bob Houston with Bob Houston eBook Formatting for facing the challenges of formatting that I am not yet ready to face.

A huge shout out especially goes to the families participating in the Spectrum Mom/Dad group on Facebook. Thank you for supporting me in this project, and for helping me gather valuable insights for the upcoming Survival Guide scheduled for release later this year.

Then, there's Bonnie (my favorite counselor of all time) who dared me to write my story. Challenge met. Thanks for being the voice of reason.

Finally, I give all my love to my children, stepchildren, daughter-in-law, parents and in-laws. And to my husband for his patience, his love, his willingness to be a stay-at-home dad when I need to recharge, and for being open to sharing our story with the world—you are truly one in a million, Frank.

About the Author

Karen Pellett is a crazy woman with a computer, and she's not afraid to use it. She was born in Utah, but over the years migrated to California, Arizona, Massachusetts, Maine, and the greater Seattle area. In the end, she returned to Utah (though her heart still resides in Seattle).

Over the years, Karen has worked as a photographer, a business analyst, and a freelance writer for newspapers and magazines. But most of her time is spent between raising three overly brilliant (and stinkin' cute) children, playing video games with her stepsons, and the rare peaceful moment with her husband. When opportunity provides she escapes to the alternate dimension to write fantasy and magical realism stories, as well as essays on raising her children on the Autism Spectrum. Karen lives, plots, writes, and hides in the suburbs of Northern Utah.

Made in the USA
Columbia, SC
21 September 2017